Spanner in the Works

Education for racial equality and social justice in white schools

IWP

Spanner in the Works

Education for racial equality and social justice in white schools

Clare Brown
Jacqui Barnfield
Mary Stone

tb

Trentham Books
Unit 13/14 Trent Trading Park, Botteslow Street,
Stoke-on-Trent ST1 3LY

First published in 1990 by Trentham Books

Reprinted 1991

Trentham Books
13/14 Trent Trading Park
Botteslow Street
Stoke-on-Trent
Staffordshire ST1 3LY
England

British Library Cataloguing in Publication Data

Brown, Clare
    Spanner in the Works: primary school teaching
    for equality and justice.
    1. Social equality
    I. Title II. Bayfield, Jacqui III. Stone, Mary
    305
    ISBN: 0-948080-38-8

Designed by Trentham Print Design Limited, Chester and printed in Great Britain by Bemrose Shafron Limited, Chester

Acknowledgements

This book is dedicated to young children in Cumbria. Through their openness and curiosity, they show us that even in the highest fell villages and the remotest towns are part of multicultural, multiracial Britain. Through their sense of justice, they demonstated again and again that every individual has a part to play in challenging inequality and working towards a more peaceful and just world.

We would like to thank the children and teachers in the following schools.

Aldingham Parochial C of E Primary
Ambleside C of E Infant
Bookwell Primary, Egremont
Bransty Primary, Whitehaven
Burneside C of E Primary
Burton Morewood Primary
Castle Park County Primary, Kendal
Cleator Moor Nursery
Dent C of E Primary
Flookburgh County Primary
Greengate Junior, Barrow
Harrington Junior, Workington
Haverigg Primary
Kendal Nursery
Kirkby Thore Primary
Lamplugh Primary
Leven Valley Primary
Milnthorpe County Primary
Montreal C of E Infant, Cleator Moor
Sandside Lodge, Special School, Ulverston
Sedbergh Primary
St George's C of E Primary, Barrow
St James' Junior C of E, Whitehaven
St Mary's Infant C of E, Windermere
St Thomas' C of E Primary, Kendal
Valley Junior, Whitehaven
Westfield Infant, Workington

We also thank the following for permission to use their material:

Beulah Candappa
Kath Pearce
Colin Smith
Theatre Centre
Whitehaven Civic Trust
Whitehaven Museum
Quaker Peace and Service
Learning Developments Aids

The following people gave us generous clerical and administrative support:

Collette Harley
Jan Dawson
Kath Rhodes

Noah Brown did the illustration on the front cover. We would like to thank him for entering so fully into the spirit of the book.

Cumbria LEA, and Denis Turner in particular, have given every encouragement to our work.

We particulary thank Gillian Klein, not only for her encouragement and constructive criticism throughout the writing of this book, but also for her conviction that the 'white highlands' can and must join the national struggle for racial equality and a just society.

The writers are:

Jacqui Barnfield, Advisory Teacher, Multicultural Education Project, Cumbria 1988-1989.

Clare Brown, Curriculum Development Officer, Multicultural Education Project 1987-1989.

Mary Stone, Former Chair, Multicultural Education Working Party 1985-1988.

Contents

SECTION I: WORKING TOWARDS SOCIAL JUSTICE

This section outlines some ideas on aspects of school life which seem to us particularly important if children are actively to work for a more just world.

SECTION II: WHOLE SCHOOL APPROACHES

The initiatives described in this section involve children in infant or junior departments or aged from 4-11. Each item goes far beyond one day or one class: all try to show how teachers are working to establish a whole school ethos.

SECTION III: THE WAY WE FEEL

This section deals with children discussing their feelings about themselves, the people around them and the world outside. By creating a space to work on issues such as differences and similarities and injustice, we hope to begin a process which will encourage children to participate in school and in the wider community as confident and questioning individuals.

SECTION IV: DIFFERENT AND THE SAME

This section describes attempts to help children to appreciate, value and cooperate with people who may appear different, rather than to allow differences to divide and separate. If children can talk openly about the differences between people and groups, they may be able to recognise how those differences can be associated with inequality and then to consider ways of challenging some of th behaviour which can lead to injustice.

SECTION V:
CONFLICTS AROUND US

Some ideas for getting into — and sometimes out of — the conflicts children experience in their daily lives are described in this section. Although the classroom work often used a picture or a story as a starting point, practically all the children wanted to discuss their own feelings.

SECTION VI:
WHAT'S IN A GANG?

This 'gang' work originated in a school in a large town in South Cumbria and involved school-based teachers and others working in multicultural, health and music education.

SECTION VII:
INSIDERS... OUTSIDERS

Local communities and people are the framework for these projects, which consider responses to 'outsiders' and how people who appear 'different' may feel.

SECTION VIII:
CHRISTIANITY AND DIVERSITY

Places of worship in Cumbria are mainly associated with one world faith — Christianity. By looking at the different ways people use churches, meeting houses etc. children can begin to develop a sense of the wide variety of religious practice in Britain and in the world.

SECTION IX:
CELEBRATIONS AND OBSERVANCES

Celebrating a festival can put children at the wrong end of a telescope, studying the 'strange habits' of people 'out there'. Here, Chinese New Year was used as an opportunity to recognise the individuality and skills of one small boy. The all-encompassing theme of light led children in South Cumbrian schools towards an appreciation of some world faiths.

SECTION X:
OTHER PEOPLE... OTHER COUNTRIES

These units attempt to explore some of the assumptions children may hold and to develop empathy with the feelings of victims of racism and other injustices.

SECTION XI:
OTHER PEOPLE... OTHER TIMES

By recreating the life of 18th Century itinerant pedlars, children in a small village school gained insight into the experiences of a group which could be regarded as 'outcasts'.

Foreword

Gerry German

This is a vivid account of how children acquire meaningful knowledge that they can use for their benefit and that of their society. It is an account also of how pupils, teachers and parents can combine their energies and interests to change the world, starting with their own institutions then, gradually, but with growing confidence, moving back the frontiers so as the embrace the locality, the region, the nation and the globe.

Britain is multi-ethnic, and has always been so. Cumbria is very much part of the richly diverse British tradition. But while British plurality is evident for those who want to see it, its pluralism has been stifled by the self-interested institution and perpetuation of class distinction, male superiority and white supremacy. If the quality of life is to improve for everybody, these myths must be challenged and exploitation and oppression resisted.

Children learn best when teachers ensure that conditions are congenial for learning and when they create a school ethos of enquiry and discovery, respect and cooperation. If the status quo doesn't seem to work for everybody, then they must turn that logic on its head and throw a spanner in the works.

If British history appears to feature only the achievements of kings and queens, capital cities far away and military conquest overseas as the epitome of human achievement, it is time that maps be redrawn, records rewritten and courses, methods and materials redesigned in order to give due credit to the achievements of ordinary people.

Spanner in the Works shows how children can themselves help to bring about change by becoming active participants in their own learning and how, as a result, classrooms, schools and whole communities become more exciting places. The children in this Cumbrian initiative are pupils in nursery, infant and primary school classes who know they are respected for what they bring to learning and how they share it with others. Because they feel assured of their place in the world, they learn to appreciate how others occupy their own spaces and how all of them can be encouraged to do so with dignity and confidence.

Unless educational institutions actively concern themselves with justice, equality and freedom, they will remain nothing more than knowledge factories instead of partnerships of learning and communities of wisdom. What Cumbria has done in this project is to release imagination and commitment and put it to work among children and adults — in the creation of a new world free from racism and other forms of oppression, and fit for all our children to live in.

I commend *Spanner in the Works* as an important contribution to the anti-racist struggle for freedom and justice world wide.

Principal Education Officer
Commission for Racial Equality

INTRODUCTION: TOWARDS EDUCATION FOR EQUALITY AND JUSTICE
Work with children aged 3-11 in Cumbria

Spanner in the Works is a record of initiatives in some nursery and primary schools in Cumbria over the last two years. The original impetus for the work was related to our Multicultural Education Project. In thinking about 'Education for All' as defined by the Swann Report (HMSO 1985), we came to believe that racism can most effectively be challenged by providing children with opportunities to discuss their own experiences and to gain a sense of themselves as participative and powerful members of communities and societies.

The *spanner* of our title emerged only towards the end of a lengthy process of evaluation and documentation of classroom work. We started collecting material for the book in 1988 and met regularly as a writing group. One of us often halted the seemingly smooth progress on the book with the cry, 'I want to throw a spanner in the works!' This spanner has become for us an important symbol:

- it took to bits our 'common sense' notions

- it unlocked a good many issues

- it wrenched open feelings about racism

- it loosened ideas about power and control in the classroom

- it tightened up our ideas about teaching for equality.

We hope that the work we describe here — developed by children and teachers in Cumbria — will provide useful reference points for others committed to exploring and developing the talents, skills and sense of justice of people in the school community.

As we have said, one focus for work towards equality and justice in Cumbria was the Multicultural Education Project. Although the Project only existed from September 1986 to March 1989, it has roots further back than that and a future into the days of the Education Reform Act.

How did we try to make sense of 'multiculturalism' in a county like Cumbria? First we had to think about who 'we' were.

Slightly less than half a million people live within our 'frontiers', perhaps five thousand of them are members of minority groups — Black, Asian and Travellers. Minority group people live dispersed in family groups throughout a county willing to accept their contribution to the economy but rarely ready to take responsibility for the occasionally savage and always harmful acts of discrimination and racism to which they are subject. The majority ethnic people of Cumbria are as diverse as one cares to perceive them. The working class communities of West Cumbria are struggling to forge a life for themselves out of a past of iron-ore, coal and steel into a future dominated by the nuclear industry. The central fells shelter strongly traditional farming communities whose relationship to the land is being questioned by considerable changes in agricultural and rural policy. The gentrified villages of the Eden valley and southern lakeland have recently seen an almost wholesale 'offcomer' of the space which only 50 years ago had a distinct Westmorland and rural identity. The two largest towns — Barrow and Carlisle — sit nearly 100 miles apart at opposite ends of the county, neither one a natural cultural or administrative centre.

Next, we needed to think about the everyday preoccupations and burning issues in Cumbria's education authority. Working within the political context of a hung council, where issues of equality and justice rarely appear on agendas; spending much of its budget on transporting children to its 340 schools — many of them with three teachers or less; involved in the relentless struggle of tiny villages to retain their schools, its apparent concerns are very different from those of, say, Camden or Coventry.

In 1984 a small group of teachers and advisers came together on the basis of their interest in widening the cultural experiences of children and, in some cases, because of their commitment to working for racial equality. They arranged a number of visits to other authorities which helped to inform the debates which continue today and are expressed in *Education for Life in a Multicultural Society*, Cumbria's Curriculum Paper Number 14 (1987).

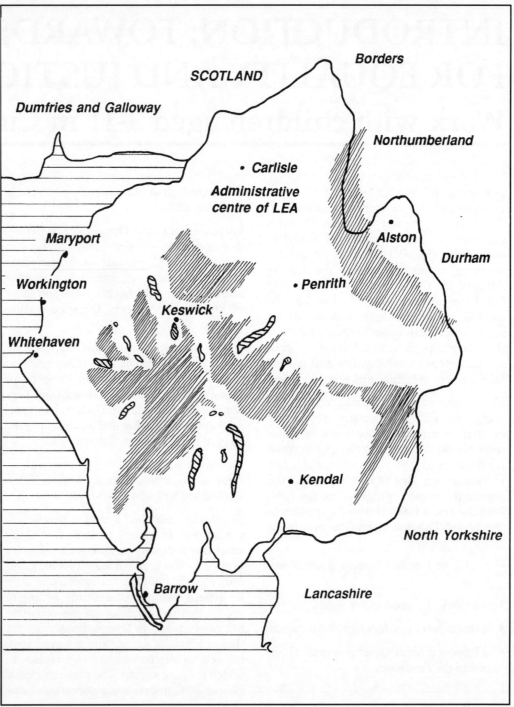

Profile of the region

Most primary schools have no minority ethnic group children

Most children have never personally known a Black or Asian person

Majority of children have no experience of living in multiracial areas

Barrow	— Carlisle	82 miles
Barrow	— Workington	59 miles
Workington	— Carlisle	33 miles
Kendal	— Carlisle	48 miles
Penrith	— Whitehaven	43 miles
Carlisle	— Manchester	118 miles
Maryport	— Newcastle	85 miles

44 secondary schools
  smallest 73 students
  largest 1160 students

317 primary schools
  smallest 11 pupils
  largest 343 pupils

We describe here some of the ideas we have discussed over the last few years. They are beginning to form a theoretical framework — still loose and sometimes wobbly! — for the work we are developing in classrooms.

- A 'cultural diversity' approach (just add on saris, samosas and steel bands!) may have a degree of success if it exposes children to the everyday experiences of individuals and thus challenges stereotypes, but must ultimately be unsuccessful if it fails to make real to children that the most oppressive form of prejudice is that which, coupled with power, results in racism.

- The notion of 'culture' as applied to black and other minority ethnic groups may itself be racist. Is there an assumption that 'they' have culture while 'we' have civilisation? (See Verity Saifullah Khan's chapter, 'The role of the culture of dominance in structuring the experience of ethnic minorities' from *Race in Britain* ed. C Husband, Hutchinson).

- The very term 'multicultural' as applied to British society post-1950 is again suspect. As many critics of the 'new history' point out, the story of Britain can always be read as the struggle of oppressed groups to gain economic power and have their cultural expression validated. To accept 'multicultural' as applicable only to some cities where there are

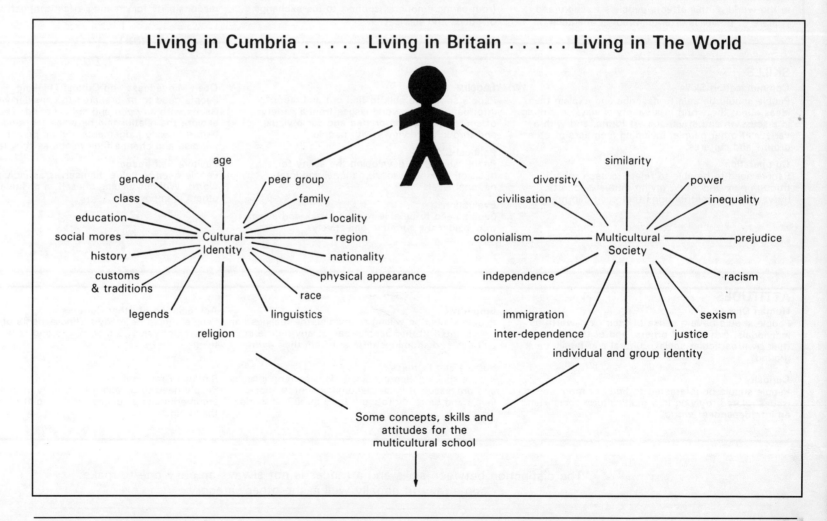

Living in Cumbria . . . . . Living in Britain . . . . . Living in The World

Cultural Identity
- age
- gender
- class
- education
- social mores
- history
- customs & traditions
- legends
- religion
- peer group
- family
- locality
- region
- nationality
- physical appearance
- race
- linguistics

Multicultural Society
- similarity
- diversity
- civilisation
- colonialism
- independence
- immigration
- inter-dependence
- power
- inequality
- prejudice
- racism
- sexism
- justice
- individual and group identity

Some concepts, skills and attitudes for the multicultural school

Some Concepts, Skills and Attitudes*

CONCEPTS

Values and Beliefs

...understanding other people's values and beliefs.
May help explain differences as well as reasons for conflict ...

Similarities and Differences

... everyone has the same basic nature... the same physical needs and similar wishes and hopes, for example for friendship, love and happiness ... We need to understand what we have in common as well as the differences.

Social Change

... while change is normal and necessary, social change can have wide ranging and complex outcomes not all of which are desirable ...

Conflict

People continually disagree and often fight with each other but the resolution of a conflict can bring people together and generate new ideas.

Power and Inequality

People or groups are able to influence what happens in the world ... this affects people's freedom and welfare ... power is often distributed unequally ...

Interdependence

People depend on each other in many ways — from caring emotional support to the exchange of goods and services.

Future

... aspirations, hopes, possibilities, probabilities .... responsibility for creating a fair and just world....

SKILLS

Communication Skills

People should be able to describe and explain their ideas about the world in a variety of ways: in writing, in discussion and in various art forms, and with a variety of other people, including members of other groups and cultures.

Co-operation

People need to be able to relate to each other through play and work, giving mutual support by valuing the contributions that each can make.

Enquiry

People should be able to find out and record information about world issues from a variety of sources, including printed and audio-visual, and through interviews with people.

Political Skills

People should be developing the ability for decision making at local, national and international levels.

Evaluation

people need to be able to stand back and attempt to consider the situation objectively.

Open-Mindedness and Critical Thinking

People need to be prepared to consider views and issues with an open and critical mind. They should explore the relationship between fact and opinion before making judgements and be prepared to compromise and change their minds as they learn more.

Positive Self-Image

People need to value themselves as individuals of worth. Without valuing oneself, a positive image of others is impossible.

ATTITUDES

Human Dignity

People should have a sense of their own worth as individuals, and that of others, and of the worth of their own particular social, cultural and family background.

Curiosity

People should be interested to find out more about issues related to living in a multicultural society and an interdependent world.

Empathy

People should be willing to imagine the feelings and viewpoints of other people, particularly people in cultures and situations different from their own.

Justice and Fairness

People should value genuinely democratic principles and processes at local, national and international levels and be ready to work for a more just world.

Appreciation of other Cultures

People should be ready to find aspects of other cultures of value to themselves and to learn from them.

Rational Argument

People need to be able to put forward reasoned arguments and evidence for the point of view they hold.

*The distinction between skills and attitudes is not always an easy one to make: some may fit equally well in the other category.

visible expressions of black experiences is to imply that there is a cultural homogeneity in the rest of Britain which ignores such vital factors as class, gender, geographical location and others.

- Even if we accepted multicultural education as simply an appreciation of the cultural experience of black and other minority ethnic groups, we would still need to take the cultural experiences of white children in any area such as ours very seriously. Cross cultural approaches such as those suggested in *Issues and Resources* (AFFOR 1983) require a careful consideration of, for example, family structures or homes in the children's own community.

- For many, if not most white children, large parts of their cultural heritage are rapidly becoming invisible as the mass media and other standardising influences distance them from their own community's traditional language forms, styles of life and sense of themselves. If children are genuinely to value, for example, the oral tradition of some Black British communities, they need to understand how similar traditions may have existed in their own communities. The issue of the cultural deprivation of large sections of the British population is one which must inform our teaching.

- If, however, we are to go beyond a cultural diversity approach and work for race equality, and if we accept that education must be genuinely child-centred, then we need to lay strong foundations in terms of a child's own felt experience so that eventually children may acquire the emotional and intellectual tools to see the connections between their own experience as more or less empowered people and the experiences of black and other minority ethnic group people.

The diagram opposite is from *Education for Life in a Multicultural Society* (Cumbria County Council. It indicates how issues of cultural identity and multicultural society can be explored in the classroom and is followed by a chart suggesting concepts, skills and attitudes for school and curriculum development.

The ideas here described have been further explored over the last few years in INSET sessions with teachers, advisers, officers and clerical and administrative staff. Although approaches in classrooms clearly vary with the ages of the children and the values and experience of the teachers, most of the steps set out below are part of the process common to all the 40 or so classes on which the book is based.

Educational approaches

- Encourage children to value themselves. Help them to see that there is beauty in people of all physical types; develop language which expresses appreciation for people seemingly very different from themselves.

- Explore with even the youngest children similarities and differences. Use the children's natural curiosity about their peers and others they see around them, to challenge ideas of what's 'normal'.

- Create a culture in the classroom which allows the children to express what they honesty feel — about themselves, the treatment they receive from and give others, their everyday conflicts and about national and international situations. Work on strategies for resolving conflict at classroom, playground and street level.

- Help children to discover aspects of their own culture, particularly those which help them to locate themselves historically, such as language forms and oral traditions, movements of people, stories about individuals or groups who have taken control over their own lives.

- Use everyday situations to analyse which people have power and influence and what 'the victims' can do to protect themselves and their rights.

- As children develop, help them to recognise which groups in society are oppressed economically and culturally, by using the tools of analysis they have developed about their own experiences.

The classroom and school work we described in this book is the product of a co-operative editing process — teachers in schools described their work to us, we wrote it down, attempted to capture the essence of what had gone on for the children, amended our drafts and suggested further work. What we present here is a series of snapshots of developing classrooms and schools. Nothing can ever be quite the same a second time around and we know that teachers using our book will take what they want from it and extend, adapt, improve ...

We offer our readers the ideas in these thirteen chapters, with the conviction that the ethos of a school is ours to create. By sharing our thoughts and feelings on teaching for equality, we will strengthen our skills for and commitment to education for all.

SECTION I:
WORKING TOWARDS SOCIAL JUSTICE

This section outlines some ideas on aspects of school life which seem to us particularly important if children are actively to work for a more just world.

Small group work

As our thinking on multicultural education developed we came to realise how critical small group work is. We needed to think through what we meant by 'small group work' because we sometimes visited schools where four or five children would be sitting around a table, all supposedly engaged on the same task but with no evidence of co-operation and collaborative learning ...

Concepts, skills and attitudes, such as co-operation, conflict, power and inequality, similarities and differences and rational argument can best be developed through active teaching and learning in small groups.

Some of the reasons for this are:

- much of our life outside school is lived in small groups and we need to understand their strengths and weaknesses;

- small groups provide a security which helps less confident pupils to express their ideas;

- small groups may help individuals to work through ideas they find hard to express in a large class (or in the teacher's presence).

- individuals may be enabled to take responsibility for helping others in the group;

- small groups may be able to help individuals to consider each other's achievements as important as their own;

- small groups make it easier to carry out co-operative tasks that require the full involvement of all;

- it is easier for a small group of individuals to appreciate that everyone's ideas need to be a part of problem solving;

- from the diversity of experience within it, a small group may find the strength and unity to work co-operatively with other very different groups;

- the strength that comes from the membership of small groups may help individuals to recognise the individuality of others and thus break down the stereotypes and prejudices often associated with inequality (such as those based on 'race').

Getting into groups

Groups of friends often sit together in classrooms. We would suggest that such groups

may not always be the best learning environment for all the children. In friendly groups, individuals may not always challenge each other or learn to support and value those with different needs and experience.

I **Random groups**

There are numerous ways of arranging a class into random groups, for example:

a) Number pupils in order, eg 1, 2, 3, 4, 1, 2, 3, 4, so that all the ones go into group one, all the twos into group two and so on (random numbering).

b) The pupils could be asked to line themselves up in age or height, after which random numbering is used. (This may help children to see that human beings can be classified in many ways.)

c) Group according to hair or eye colour. (Ask the children how they feel about this sort of grouping!)

d) Put different coloured paper on the floor or in parts of the room and have the children move to their favourite colour or to the colour which matches an item of their clothing.

e) Cut up some old Christmas/birthday cards, into 3/4/5 pieces and put them

in a bag/box. Each pupil picks a piece and then matches it with others, like a jigsaw, until they make the whole card. (This encourages discussion even before the group work begins.)

f) Animal Farm: Choose a number of animals — cat, dog, pig, cow, sheep — depending on how many people you want per group and make cards with each animal's name on (eg 5 cat cards, 5 dog cards etc). Mix them up like a pack of cards. Before giving one card to each pupil explain that once they get a card they cannot speak. On the word 'Go', the pupils must make the animal's noise and join up with others who are also mewing, barking or whatever, until they have located all their members. Rather noisy but lots of fun!

g) Give each child the name of a fruit — oranges, peaches, pears, mangoes. Ask each child to join together with different fruits to make a fruit salad (more kinds of fruit will make larger groups).

II Teacher engineered groups

a) Sometimes teachers may want two or more children to work together for a particular reason. For example in a project on Hanukah — a winter festival of light — the teacher wanted the two most articulate children to work together so that they could challenge each other's ideas.

b) There are occasions when teachers will choose to organise the class into girls' and boys' discussion groups. The issues discussed may well be identical but both girls and boys sometimes need to gain clarity and strength from those who share their experiences before they can contribute fully to a mixed discussion.

III Free choice work

There may be times when friendship groups are a good forum for initial work. For example, issues related to cultural diversity are sometimes best dealt with in groups where the children can explore the feelings of their friends *before* children can approach with sensitivity people they may not know so well. (In recent work on language and dialect, pupils felt most comfortable initially discussing their feelings with their friends.)

Other considerations

1. Establish, and periodically review 'ground rules', so that children and teachers are clear about the responsibilities they have towards each other. Defining good rules is itself an excellent small group activity. Some of the areas to be considered could be:

   • How can we make sure everyone is listened to?

   • What could we do if one of the group members behaves badly?

   • What happens when some people work more quickly than others?

   • How can we let the teacher know when we're ready?

2. *Be flexible.*
The children's responses may mean that the teacher has to change direction, in order to capitalise on what the children offer. (See, for example, VI, 20 *Names and Name Calling*.)

3. *Try to show that you have a high expectation of group work.*
The teacher could tell the children that if they work individually they can come up with good ideas but 3 or 4 working together produce a result that exceeds the parts.

4. *Try to show that a co-operative exercise has many advantages.*
The teacher can explain that, in order to get the very best answer, everyone needs to be listened to. Each contribution needs to be discussed and then a group decision can be made based on the fullest available knowledge.

5. *Try to make sure that any individual pupils with difficulties are taken care of within the group.*
This grows and develops as the group learns to take on board responsibility for all members of the group.

6. *Encourage pupils:*
   i) *to experiment with negotiation;*
   Roles can be negotiated within the group. Try to ensure that there are enough jobs so that all have a role and that roles are regularly changed so that power is shared.
   For example, a pupil who always leads can be encouraged to listen or observe, whilst a quiet pupil takes a leadership role.

   ii) *to take risks;*
   The teacher and pupils need to accept all contributions seriously. Group work should encourage all children to speculate and experiment. An idea which might appear outrageous when voiced to the whole class might germinate and take flight in a small group.

7. *Care needs to be taken so that a group member is not blamed if the group fails.*
Make it clear at the outset that no one person has total responsibility, so that the success or failure is shared. (It's not necessarily wrong to fail.)

Ways of using books

2

Introduction

The staff of a two teacher school in a remote Dales village requested the loan of a box of story books from the Schools' Library Service. They particularly asked for stories reflective of a range of cultures and countries. The books remained in the school for six weeks and were taken home by all the children. In discussion with the children, the teacher discovered how much they had enjoyed reading them and having access to so many 'new' books. However, they were concerned that no child had commented on the cultural and racial diversity the books reflected. On discussing this with an advisory teacher, both teachers said they didn't know where to start using books to talk about cultural diversity. The advisory teacher undertook to provide a framework for using books to discuss cultural diversity and, more importantly, to suggest how images might be used to challenge attitudes.

The central question seemed to be:-

i)   What role ought teachers to play in raising awareness of differences?

ii) How can teachers raise awareness of issues connected with 'race' and culture without confirming stereotypes?

iii) When and how might teachers use books to challenge prejudice?

This chapter offers some suggestions for using books as active agents for multicultural education.

A. General guidelines

1. There should always be the underlying idea of appreciating the differences between people as well as the similarities. This can refer to physical appearance, feelings, interests, behaviour and experiences. We need to project positive images of all people.

2. The terms 'black people'* and 'white people' are to be preferred. We may discuss why no term is accurate. If we add the word 'people' to the adjective, the emphasis is on the humanity of all. We should discuss with children the inaccuracy of mere terms and the importance of referring to people in the way they themselves choose. Point out when there are black people and white people in the story and draw attention to the fact that there are black people and white people in Britain and in the world. If white primary age children do not encounter books with black characters in them, then their stereotyped images are found to be very strong at secondary age. They become resistant to books featuring black characters.

* We use "black people" to refer to the section of the British population of New Commonwealth and Pakistani origin, that is the population born in New Commonwealth countries and Pakistan and their children born here. Used thus, this term does not imply a cultural homogeneity among the various groups to which it refers. 'Black' is often used as a political term to describe those discriminated against on grounds of colour and/or ethnicity.

Recently the Commission for Racial Equality has suggested that it may be more appropriate to refer to non-white minority groups as 'black' or 'Asian'.

3. Try to use and appreciate books which show traditional artwork of different cultures.

4. Encourage children to identify with the experiences and feelings that are common to all human beings. (See, for example, *Myself, I'm Special*, ACER.)

5. In their concern that children respect each other, teachers are sometimes uncomfortable about pointing out differences. However, differences *do* exist and may be reflected in books. The research shows that children perceive such differences as readily as adults. Unless children can learn to understand and respect what makes us different from each other, they will tend to cope with their own confusions and fear by name calling and even bullying. If we ignore the realities of difference then children may suffer. For

example, where teachers avoided drawing attention to difference, it led to the following two incidents:

i)   A black child was persistently called 'chocolate drop' in the playground.

ii) A child suffering from leukaemia who returned to school after receiving chemotherapy was called 'baldy'.

Giving children positive ways of thinking about differences and dealing with their possible insecurities and fears of the 'new' enables them to handle potentially threatening situations.

Approaches

1) Read a *story* early in the school day rather than in the last ten minutes to allow time for important, detailed discussion.

2) With *picture story books* the issues generally develop in stages. The teacher reads the book to the children more than once. On first reading, the story will probably be paramount. During subsequent readings, the children or teacher may raise issues:

eg

How do you think that person feels?
Have you ever felt like that?
How could you help him/her?
What makes people the same?
What makes people different?

Children can be encouraged to consider whether or not the people in the book reflect their experience of real people or whether they are portrayed in a stereotyped way. The teacher may ask, for example:

Are all grannies like that?
Do you know mothers who don't do that?

3) *Longer stories.* Teachers will want to choose books with positive images of black people and minority ethnic group people. Allow time and space for the children to reflect on and discuss issues as they arise.

4) *Children reading to themselves.* Teachers can encourage children to describe and comment on what has happened in the story so far. This creates the opportunity for discussion of stereotypes and negative remarks either with the reader or, occasionally, with the whole group.

5) *Responding to children's comments.* When children are encouraged to make comments, these may be negative. (See 'Teaching About Race' by Stuart Hall: *Multicultural Education* 9(1) Autumn 1980) The teacher may believe it healthy to bring these feelings out into the open so that they can be discussed. If, however, there are black children in the class, the teacher needs to consider how they might feel during such a discussion. Whilst challenging racist language and behaviour, teachers have a particular responsibility for the well-being of isolated black children.

For example, a six year old child dismissed a character in a book by saying:

Oh, he's just a blackie.

The teacher did not know what to say, if anything. On reflection she felt that this derogatory comment required discussion. Before reading the story again

she prepared her strategy with questions such as:

Why do you say that?
How might the boy in the story feel if he heard you say that about him?
How would you feel?
What names don't you like to be called?

It is advisable for the discussion to be guided throughout by the teacher.

B.   Some books found useful for deepening understanding

Accounts of children's experiences of black family life in Britain

Eat up Gemma by Sarah Hayes, Walker Books

Happy Christmas Gemma by Sarah Hayes, Walker Books

Carry, Go, Bring, Come by Yvanne Samuels, Bodley Head

Bet you can't by Penny Dale, Bodley Head

Ming's Surprise by Stephanie Harris Lang, Headstart story book.

Stories, Folk Tales, Traditional Stories and Myths

The main emphasis is likely to be on the enriching quality of cultural diversity. You may look at universal themes, eg good and evil, that children are familiar with and can compare with stories from other cultures. Look again for similarities and differences.

The Village of Round and Square Houses by A Grifalconi, Methuen

Mufaro's Beautiful Daughter by J Steptoe, Hamish Hamilton

Amoko and Efua Bear by S Appiah, Andre Deutsch

Lord of the Dance by V Tadjo, A& C Black

Kapiti Plain by Verna Aardema, Macmillan

Caribbean Canvas by F Lessac, Macmillan

Imagine That! by S and S Corrin, Puffin

Books about Black People in other Countries

Before using these books make it clear that a book is about only the people featured and is only the author's perception.

Use the idea: How might we show other people what our village/town is like, using only six photographs?

The Perfect Present (Barbados) by R and N Thomson, A and C Black

Whatever Next (Trinidad) by R and N Thomson, A and C Black

Very Special Sari (India) by F Matheson, A and C Black

Lost at the Fair (India) by F Matheson, A and C Black

Underground to Canada by Barabara Smucker, Puffin

Lost in Town by P Bonnici, Hodder and Stoughton

The Special Event by P Bonnici, Hodder and St oughton

The Village Show by P Bonnici, Hodder and Stoughton

These last three books feature families in India and Britain who write to each other about their countries. They show that both countries are multicultural and multiracial, have urban and rural communities, rich and poor people, mixed race families and followers of different religions.

Themes

Take a theme and explore it across 'races' and cultures beginning with the children's own experience. Emphasise that people of different cultures have, for example, ways of dressing their hair to look attractive. Appreciate different amounts of time and skill involved.

Everybody's Hair by J Solomon, A and C Black

Friends by Chris Deshpande, Black

Finger Foods by Chris Deshpande, Black

Five Stones and Knuckle Bones by Chris Deshpande, Black

Scrape, Rattle and Blow by Chris Deshpande, Black

Starting School by J and A Ahlberg, Viking Kestrel

Books showing people of different 'races' and cultures working together and some of the issues that may arise.

Encourage children to use positive language about physical features.

But Martin by June Counsel, Faber and Faber

(All the above books are in Cumbria's School Library Service.)

To find out about more books that are suitable, teachers could consult:

1) Books for Keeps Guides by Judith Elkin.

2) 'Review Roundup in summer issue — each year — of Multicultural Teaching.

3) Letterbox Library

Questions that might be used

Example A

Would You Rather ...? by J Burningham

On the page where dad is dancing in the classroom, ask the children:

> How would you feel if that was your dad?
> How might other children feel?

If you felt you could use the book with older children you might ask:

Some people say that red-headed people lose their tempers and that boys don't show their feelings? What do you think?

Example B

Maybe It's a Tiger by Kathleen Herson, Picture Macs

The early pages show children playing on the steps. Ask the children:

> What have they been doing?
> What are they feeling?
> How do you know?

The teacher needs to ensure that children understand that black people and white people often have similar feelings.

> What kind of place do they live in?

Look for similarities and differences.

> Where do they all live?
> Why do you think so?
> Why is one wearing a hat?
> Who is looking after the baby?
> Who would use the skateboard?
> What is your favourite game?
> Is it best when grown-ups join in or when they don't?

Example C

But Martin ... by June Counsel, Faber and Faber

This book, which was used in nursery and infant classes, stimulated much discussion in a group of teachers. No teacher would raise all these questions with one group of children but they do show what is possible.

page 2 (Angela crying):

> How do you feel when you come to school?
> How could we help Angela?

page 3 Decide on names, feelings, look at the faces and the body language:

> What is different about each character?
> What are they wearing?
> What colour are their skins?
> Do you know people who have a different colour skin to yours?
> Have you seen people of a different colour to you on T.V?
> What makes people different?
> What makes people the same?

page 4/5 (Martin in spacecraft):

> What's Martin like?
> How might he feel?

page 6/7 (Characters' faces) Look for similarities and differences.

page 8/9 Describe Martin:

> How might Martin feel?

page 10/11 Ask children to compare the feel of each other's hair. Make a positive statement about them all.

page 14/15 (Characters' reactions to Martin are negative):

> How would Martin feel?
> What could the children have said?

page 16 Why did Martin bleep and not talk?

page 19 Discuss the characters' reaction to the bell.

> Guess what Martin would do now.

page 20 What would the children think and do when Martin vanished?

page 21 Looking at the faces of the four characters coming into school

> How do they feel?
> Would Martin come?

page 22 Could the other children come through the wall?

page 23 (Characters working at their desks?):

> Could they do all their work?

page 24/25 (Martin knew everything)

> Could he help them?

page 26/27 (Martin worked out his answers in his head. He helped them):

> Were they pleased?

page 28/29 (Martin wrote well)

> How did the children feel?

page 30/31 (Going home.) Discuss means of transport and compare with their own.

> Guess how Martin went home.

Possible points for general discussion:
> Were all the children the same?
> In what ways were they similar?
> In what ways were they different?
> What does it feel like to be different?
> Does it matter being different?
> How do we show that we are friendly towards somebody who we think is different?

Note on self-image

Throughout this discussion on the use of *But Martin* there is an underlying assumption that *all* children need to feel good about themselves in order to develop positive ways of behaving towards those perceived to be different. Much has been written about the self-image of black children: white children also need to shed some of their cultural inheritance, which allows praise for only certain physical attributes and certain types of behaviour.

3

'Pole Pole' — an approach to twinning

Introduction

'Pole Pole' is the Swahili for go very slowly (pronounced poli poli)

There is no one ideal recipe for successful twinning. There are identifiable ingredients, though, points that need to be considered, that are inter-related and multi-faceted. The following have been gathered from experience in a number of Cumbrian schools.

They should be of use to any school considering a twinning project. Such a project needs to be thought of in terms of years rather than weeks or months. You won't get much benefit if you start with 10-11 year olds. Both schools should be very clear, and wholly agreed, about the aims.

Aims: to develop the following Concepts, Skills and Attitudes:

- valuing one's own culture and environment by sharing positive aspects of it with other children

- challenging stereotypes about people of different cultures and races

- appreciating the views of other children

- understanding similarities, that is, that all human beings have the same basic nature and the same physical and emotional needs

- appreciating the different ways in which human needs are met

- understanding something of the diversity that exists in British society today

- developing self-worth and valuing others

- encouraging and helping to facilitate friendships between children as equals

- developing curiosity and open-mindedness, so that children are prepared to consider different views

- learning the meaning of co-operation by working together at common tasks

- developing empathy so as to enter into the feelings of others

1. **What it takes — from the staff of both schools**

   i) A whole school approach — especially if the next year's class teachers are to build on the children's experiences.

   ii) A real sense of commitment — and teachers most deeply involved should realise that outcomes may be long-term.

   iii) A sense of humour.

   iv) Good relations between teachers from both schools, and full involvement from the outset. (Some of the most successful links are between schools where staff already knew each other.)

   v) Time for the participating teachers from both schools to meet, preferably to work together in advance in each other's school.

   vi) Not seeing difficulties as threats — overcoming them is a way of promoting harmony and co-operation.

   vii) Time to develop programmes of work suitable for both groups of children so that all are enriched by the twinning.

   viii) Active involvement of both headteachers — this enhances the value of the work in the eyes of children, parents, staff, governors and the community.

The 'Staff Survival Kit for Twinning' opposite just about sums it up!

2. **Time scale**

There are no hard and fast rules. We would advocate that children's first experience of twinning should be with a neighbouring school; perhaps in the next village or the other side of town, so that children can appreciate the similarities and differences that exist and share common experiences. This will help to prepare them for the challenges posed by linking with a school that has greater cultural diversity.

If the initial linking is with 7 and 8 year olds, there will be time during the next few

STAFF SURVIVAL KIT FOR TWINNING

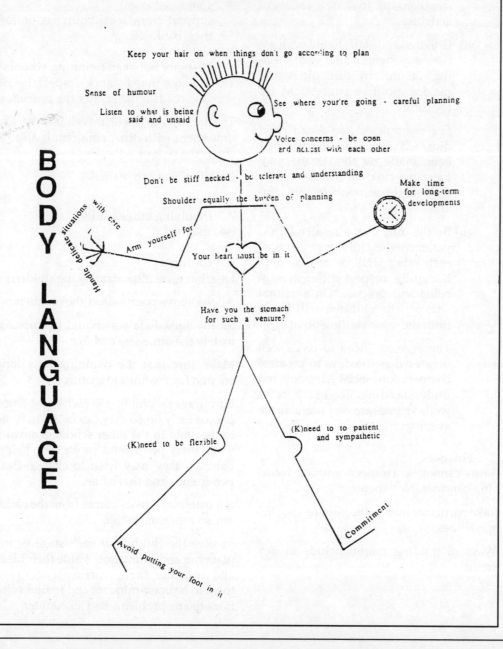

Keep your hair on when things don't go according to plan

Sense of humour

Listen to what is being said and unsaid

See where you're going - careful planning

Voice concerns - be open and honest with each other

Don't be stiff necked - be tolerant and understanding

Shoulder equally the burden of planning

Make time for long-term developments

Handle delicate situations with care

Arm yourself for

Your heart must be in it

Have you the stomach for such a venture?

(K)need to be flexible

(K)need to to patient and sympathetic

Avoid putting your foot in it

Commitment

BODY LANGUAGE

---

years to develop links in a carefully structured manner.

The time scale *might* look like this:

> 7-8 year olds: twin with a neighbouring school
> 8-9 year olds: continue the contact
> or: link with a different type of school in Cumbria eg urban with rural, or primary with special
> 9-10 year olds: twin with a school with a greater cultural diversity
> 10-11 year olds: continue this link and include a residential experience.

3. Approaches

Whatever the type of twinning, the approaches are similar:

i) *Start small with letter writing*. Exchange information eg about oneself, one's hobbies and interests, description of home and school. Send photos, tapes and videos etc and ask questions of the other children. All the work needs to be vetted by the teacher before being posted, for example, the letter to a child born in Britain, asking how often she went home (to the Caribbean).

ii) *A day's outing*. Meet on neutral ground to share some activity. Teachers in both schools need to have agreed what the appropriate challenges and learning experiences are for each group of children. In a Cumbrian/Lancashire twinning experience, an outdoor education session was planned to enable children to work together — and only afterwards was it appreciated that children from a largely Muslim school had different experiences of and attitudes to outdoor education.

iii) *Continue corresponding*. Personal friendships may arise out of this joint visit.

iv) *A residential experience* may be arranged for groups of children from each school. The first such meeting needs to be on neutral ground so that both groups are learning together in a new situation and neither group has background knowledge. Again, staff must be in agreement as to the shared learning experiences.

4. Visits

i) Schools may take it in turn to organise the details of each shared experience, although it is advisable for schools initially to consult each other.

ii) Meetings on neutral ground prevent either class from feeling at a disadvantage. It also avoids the 'zoo' or 'goldfish bowl' effect.

iii) If children have written to each other on several occasions and sent photos of themselves, their families, their school, then by the time they meet, they will feel that they already 'know' each other, so lessening initial strain or reticence.

iv) 'Ice-breaker' activities in small groups will also help break down shyness at the first meeting (see Resources list for ice-breaker books).

v) It has been found that if only a third or a half of each class meet at one time, the numbers are more manageable, the children feel less overwhelmed and of more account. If it's impossible to avoid taking a whole class, split it up into small groups, to share a variety of activities.

vi) Children and staff should evaluate their experiences after each meeting, facing any difficulties and making positive suggestions for the future.

For example, a non-Asian child didn't like the sweets that had been made by the Asian child. Later the children discussed how they might respond to this situation.

vii) By the time of the residential experience, the children will know each other well, be at ease and, hopefully, respect differences in belief and practice. On a neutral site, all the children will begin from the same starting point.

The evenings need to be as well organised as the days to promote co-operation, social harmony and understanding. Ice-breakers as well as games are very useful in the evenings.

5. Finance
Visits cannot be arranged without incurring considerable expense.

Take particular note of the most recent DES guidelines.

Ways of funding might include money from:

capitation
area inspector/adviser
school fund
PTA
sponsored event
support from local churches, industries, banks etc.

6. Distance between twinning schools
The greater the distance (especially on winding roads!), the greater the problems.

The more time spent travelling, the less time spent with other children. It also restricts the type of activities possible.

Children may arrive tired.

7. Involving other adults
(see diagram)

8. Children
Last, but most important — the children.

All the above points affect the children.

Ideally, linked classes should be approximately the same size and age.

Make sure that the twinning lasts long enough for the links to mature.

Encourage the children to exchange named photos early on so they can begin to write to the child in the other school. Knowing what their pen-friend looks like helps. Later on they may wish to change their pen-friends and that's fine.

If the desire to 'twin' comes from the children, so much the better.

Involve the children at each stage of the planning and evaluation. Value their ideas and consider their worries. Encourage them to be open-minded, and to find solutions to any problems they encounter.

INVOLVING OTHER ADULTS

(Draw on the experiences and expertise of other adults)

1) Keep parents and governors fully informed.

2) Involve as many of them as possible in the actual visits - they become our best ambassadors for the work in which we are involved.

3) Invite parents and governors into school to see the work the children have done/are doing.

4) Report regularly eg. governor's meetings

5) Keep your area inspector/adviser informed. You may need his/her moral support, financial support ... ideas ...

PARENTS →   ← **GOVERNORS**

OTHER ADULTS INVOLVED

ANCILLARY STAFF

People such as caretakers, kitchen staff, playground helpers, need to be fully informed, sympathetic and encouraged to be actively supportive.

OTHERS

Visits might involve others:

bus drivers
students
staff of places to be visited
travellers to and from other lands
CEO
Local media

CONTACTS

Have any other nearby schools twinning experience?
Learn from them.

---

9. Resources

Kendal Multicultural Project booklet.

Examples of twinning experiences ..
Burneside/Vickertown
Castle Park/Rochdale
St Thomas' Kendal/Old Hutton
Alfred Barrow/Wolverhampton.

'Words and Faces'
Afro-Caribbean Education Resource Centre (ACER), Wyvil School, Wyvil Road, London SW8 2TJ

Ice-breaker activities ...

'Youth Games Handbook' A Dearling and H Armstrong, I T Resources Centre.

'Games for Social Skills' Tim Bond, Hutchinson

'Some of the ways our thinking has developed' — Staff Development in a nursery school

Background

A nursery school in a market town in south Cumbria with 132 children on roll.

1. Staff meetings:

On returning from meetings or courses, it's customary to share what the staff have learned, both formally and informally as appropriate. The informal discussions usually take place during lunch break.

More formal staff meetings are of two types: the regular full length, after-school staff meetings for which an agenda has been prepared, and secondly, a short information-giving session before school each Friday morning.

2. Staff responses:

A member of staff attended a three-day course on multicultural education and at the next staff meeting the headteacher initiated discussion about the school's philosophy, which she felt ought to include a multicultural dimension.

There were three types of reaction:

i) Staff who were very uneasy kept silent.

ii) Those who were hesitant made negative comments, which included: *I can see what's going to happen ... We've enough on our plates without adding anything else...*

We've already a school full of first rate library books ...

iii) Some staff felt sufficiently secure to voice their doubts about making changes: *I agree with what you're saying but it won't be easy.*

On reflection, the staff realised that these three reactions were stages which they needed to work through before they could effect change.

This was their first step along the road to introducing a multicultural perspective into their school policy and practice.

3. Self worth.

The head tried to ensure that the staff were aware of how she valued them and respected their judgement, even though there were times when she did not share their views. Through discussion they became increasingly aware that unless people — children, parents and staff — have a feeling of self-worth, they are unlikely to have respect for others. As a result they all made a concentrated effort to be positive and appreciative in all their dealings with children, parents and each other. They used positive language about negative behaviour.

For example ... 'Please walk in the classroom' ... replaced 'Don't run'.

4. Positive images about people from our multi-ethnic society.

The broader concepts of multicultural education were implicit in the school's declared ethos:

Developing a child's self confidence, Home-School links,

and now:

Recognising and appreciating the cultural diversity within Cumbria.

The staff believe that they are now more able to focus their thinking on multi-ethnic aspects and realise that for three and four year olds it has to begin with real experience.

For instance they provided dolls which reflected the diversity of people in Britain and took any opportunity that arose for discussing similarities and differences.

One day a child threw a 'black' doll across the 'house' saying:

We don't want this rubbish.

The teacher picked up the doll and cuddled it. The boy said he did not like the colour of the doll's hair. The teacher took the boy to a mirror and talked about his hair, which was ginger, and said:

Is your hair different from mine? What colour is it?

The teacher continued:

I like your hair even though it's a different colour from mine and I still like the doll's hair, although she is a different colour from you and me.

Gradually the child was beginning to see that one does not have to reject something just because it's different. Although we recognise that the roots of racism are not, in the end, concerned with physical attributes but with economic and power systems, we believe that it's important for children, from an early age, to appreciate and value differences.

This teacher was dealing with racism and the staff use such 'incidental' occasions gently to help the children appreciate that all people are of equal worth, and that they may differ in many ways.

This incident indicated that teachers need to provide Afro-Caribbean and Asian dolls as well as white ones, so that children have an opportunity to explore their feelings. It showed the teachers how important work on race relations is for the early years.

The staff realised that they are all at different stages in their own understanding and will continue to find some situations difficult to handle. They feel they can now discuss these and learn from each other. They also agree that change has to come slowly or it may become counterproductive. They continue to learn from each experience.

The staff make the most of any visitors. For instance, a visitor from Hong Kong showed the children Chinese pottery, and wrote some words with Cantonese characters which he then spoke. A teacher recorded these on tape. The children were fascinated; their positive reactions are shown in such remarks as:

I'm just going to do some Albert writing.
I wish I was a little Chinese girl.

There were other comments too:

I'm never going to China.
I don't like Chinese food.

This followed a Chinese cooking session of bean sprouts, whole grain rice and soya sauce. The children ate the food with chop sticks made from scalded twigs they had collected.

There were many positive responses from parents after the Chinese New Year celebrations and this encouraged the staff to see the value of a multicultural dimension to their work.

5. The curriculum

The staff discussed how introducing a multicultural dimension was more a matter of shifting perspective than devising a new area of the curriculum. When they looked at their syllabi they saw that some areas lent themselves to an appreciation of cultural diversity.

Such as:

food ... different kinds of bread
festivals ... of light, Christmas, Divali and Hannukah;
family holidays ... parents brought back photographs, dolls, food and clothes. The teachers used these to encourage the children to appreciate different lifestyles;
home corner ... furnishings and dressing up clothes.

With these starting points, the staff feel more confident and able to explore the multicultural aspect of every topic.

6. Home-school liaison.

This has always been of the utmost importance. The staff are concerned lest families feel threatened by the school's activities, so the nursery staff keep parents fully informed about what goes on and encourage parents to be involved in the school.

Recently, a mother went into school to put her daughter's name on the waiting list. The child was of mixed race. The mother asked how the philosophy of the school would enable her daughter to settle and ensure that she did not suffer from name-calling and abuse. A real challenge in an all-white school. But at least the first steps have already been taken.

Working together

Background

A teacher in a village primary school was horrified by the attitude of her class to a local person with severe learning difficulties. He was regularly seen around and about in the village, and the children wasted no opportunity to call him names and poke fun at him.

In order to challenge her class's attitude the teacher started to work with a local special school, involving her six and seven year olds and the eight year olds with severe learning difficulties in the special school.

Aims: to develop the following Concepts, Skills and Attitudes:

an understanding that:

- everyone is different and yet we all have similar needs

- we are interdependent

- we all need care and emotional support

- promoting co-operation through work and play

- helping children to combat their preconceptions about other children with severe learning difficulties

- helping 'normal' children to use an opportunity to talk to their peers who may look 'normal' but might display anti-social habits, whose speech they might find unintelligible and whose behaviour

and ideas they might sometimes find bizarre

- helping children develop a positive self-image

- helping children to channel their curiosity about differences

- helping children to challenge prejudice at an early age

- helping children to develop harmonious relationships.

Process:

1. Introduction

The two schools have used a variety of approaches and strategies to try to establish a successful, working link that would prove exciting and beneficial to all concerned. The teachers from both schools had learnt that the younger the children, the greater the chance of success, as illustrated by an earlier experience with teenagers from the special school who had been involved in a dance project with the primary school. The nine and ten year olds from the primary school were reluctant to touch the teenagers, many of whom were less physically co-ordinated, although a picnic for both groups appeared more successful.

In any such meeting, the adults need to have considered how much verbal and physical contact will be demanded, so that children are challenged but protected. The dance workshop and the picnic had raised

issues about the feelings of both groups of children. Both sets of teachers felt that a first meeting needs to be carefully structured in order to protect all the children.

At all stages the commitment of the staff, the heads and the rest of the school, including the ancillary workers, was a crucial factor.

2. Eight children from the special school worked in the village primary school alongside eight infant children for one morning a week for six weeks, in creative and expressive arts. It was felt that this went some way to establishing more understanding between the groups, because it required the children to share ideas and resources.

On one occasion the group were told the story of 'The Gingerbread Man', after which they worked in mixed groups to create the characters. They used paint, fabric, wool, paper and a variety of other materials to depict the man, the woman, the fox, ... These pictures were shared with the rest of the class and were much admired.

3. Only at this point did the teachers feel that the children were ready to spend whole days in each other's company. This was arranged for one day a week for two children from the special school, who followed the normal curriculum, and were encouraged to mix at playtime and to join in the queues at lunchtime.

Integration was easier for Michelle, perhaps because she could converse with the others. Stuart's speech was not understood by the children and they were wary of his physically demonstrative actions.

As the weeks progressed, the relationships were built and strengthened. Parents who worked in the classroom were also involved and told other parents what was happening, which enhanced the project.

Michelle wanted to go to the school in her ordinary clothes and not in what she considered her school uniform, so that she would be like the children in the infant class.

Michelle and Stuart worked in different groups during the day, in a variety of activities including a science/CDT project. Their group was to make something that rolled; so they designed and made a moving vehicle. Throughout the task Michelle and Stuart were fully involved and treated as valued members of their group, and the project was successfully completed.

At one stage the children made a video of a PE session. They all used the large apparatus. When Stuart was having problems with balance, one of the infant children went across to lend assistance without being asked to do so. This incident passed unnoticed at the time and would have remained hidden had not the video recorded for the staff what had happened.

If for any reason the two children didn't turn up to lessons, the class wanted to know where they were and why they weren't coming.

At a govenors' meeting in the primary school, the teacher was asked whether the infant class gained anything from the venture. She replied very positively — that they had developed some understanding of physical and mental disability, and had begun to learn not to be afraid, or judgemental.

Future work

The children from the primary school had begun to develop positive attitudes towards others with learning difficulties.

As a next step, they might begin to look at the way that we create unequal opportunities for some groups in society. See the chapters on:

Conflict resolution ... Using a picture.
Who listens?

SECTION II:
WHOLE SCHOOL APPROACHES

The initiatives described in this section involve children in infant or junior departments or aged from 4-11. Each item goes far beyond one day or one class: all try to show how teachers are working to establish a whole school ethos.

The storyteller

6

Background

The school serves a small rural community in West Cumbria. Its 31 pupils are drawn from nearby villages and isolated farms. The infant class in which this project took place has 15 children whose ages range from 4-7 years.

Aims: to develop the following Concepts, Skills and Attitudes:

- **awareness** of stories about different life styles, cultures and settings (the stories to form the basis for language and art work)

- **awareness** of cultural diversity through the medium of story

- **caring** and sharing (these were a basis for several assemblies)

- **understanding** the effects of exploitation

- **understanding** that human beings share the same basic needs, concerns and similar forms of expression, such as rhymes, chants and stories

- challenging the stereotyping already apparent in the class by inviting a highly skilled story teller from another ethnic background.

Process

1. Inviting the storyteller, Beulah Candappa

The local college of education organised a story-telling festival and the school requested a visit from Beulah Candappa, a practising teacher and author.

2. Visual impact

The children entered the classroom where Beulah had created a setting using hangings and artifacts. These included the familiar — a Welsh dragon and characters from British nursery rhymes, as well as objects which were completely unfamiliar and unexpected. The children's eyes lit up at the display and at the smiling face of the visitor. She made eye contact with all the children before she began. She greeted them by putting her hands together and slightly bowing over them, and taught them how to reply. From the very beginning she

showed them respect and expected to be treated with respect herself.

3. Starting with the familiar

Beulah started with nursery and clapping rhymes that the children knew. She then introduced an unfamiliar action rhyme about crocodiles, and went on to tell some stories. These stories were always interspersed with rhymes which the children chose and sang. The variety of material was considerable, and there was always a balance between what was known and the fascinatingly unfamiliar.

Every so often she allowed the children time to wriggle about and get comfortable again before she proceeded. She made it very clear, in a friendly way, when it was time to be still. She used recorded music to help create the mood, recorded the children's singing and played them tapes of other children's singing. She gave them the impression that they were performing for a wider audience than herself; that children in other schools would hear their tape.

Throughout the session, Beulah was prepared to listen to her audience and they were most attentive to her. They were entranced throughout and at the end went out very quietly to the music that she played.

4. The themes which link people
Beulah showed how many of the rhymes, chants and stories from different countries cover similar themes, for example, a cruel step-mother; or how good overcomes evil.

5. Challenging stereotypes
One child, who had previously used racist language, treated this person of a different colour with great suspicion and sat himself down as far away from her as possible. As the afternoon progressed, his suspicion evaporated and his interest in and acceptance of her increased. This was evident by the way he edged nearer to her and ended up with his elbow on her knee.

The teacher had never witnessed such a change in a child during one afternoon. Eight months later, he still recalls the rhymes and stories with delight, remembering every detail.

This is a child who had never shown any interest in books and reading but during the session he wanted to know all about the books she had brought with her that she had written herself (See Resources). He was very anxious for reassurance that he would have access to them after she'd left.

6. Since her visit, the school has purchased the two sets of books written by Beulah Candappa.

7. The books prompted the children to write their own stories for children in a neighbouring school. They took seriously the idea that they were authors, writing a description of themselves just inside their 'books', considering layout, illustrations, a publisher's logo, and even the price!

8. The children learnt some of the rhymes in the books. For example, *Bharunda Bird* (© Beulah Candappa) below.

Further work
The teachers are now looking for other visitors to enrich the children's experience and challenge their stereotypes.

Where to look for visitors
i) Contact any local community organisation or mosque, synagogue, gurdwara, church ...

ii) In seemingly 'white' areas, ask local people, such as British Asian doctors or nurses and teachers.

iii) Encourage a local college to hold storytelling festivals.

iv) Ask local organisations such as Oxfam or Save the Children Fund to let the school know when visitors from black and minority ethnic groups are in the area.

Resources
Tales from the Far East and *Tales of South Asia* by Beulah Candappa. 360 Reading Scheme level 10 Ginn

---

<u>The Bharunda Bird</u>.

The Bharunda bird can teach us why,

We should care for each other
or wither and die,

One life, one world, that's all we've got,

So share with each other,
Don't <u>grab</u> the lot.

Indian Dance: Enriching the curriculum

Background

The primary school, with 150 on roll, is part of a small industrial community surrounded by traditional lakeland countryside.

Aims: to develop the following Concepts, Skills and Attitudes:

developing the skills of:

- relating to and working with people from a different background

- using classical Indian dance to enrich curricular areas and themes

- meeting Asian people as professionals coming into school with skills.

Teachers in the school place great emphasis on the concepts, skills and attitudes which underpin multicultural education, for example, co-operation, conflict resolution and challenging prejudice. There is a feeling, however, that multicultural education should also provide children with the opportunity to meet and work with black individuals. The school's strong tradition of dance meant that work with Indian dancers could take forward multicultural work while the children used a new dance form to explore curriculum areas. The headteacher is influenced by the work of Dartington Hall, the Arts and Education Centre in Devon which has developed ideas which link British work on child development with Indian philosophy, particularly that of Rabindranath Tagore. Following these ideas on self-concept and creativity, introducing classical Indian dance as a means of interpretation was a natural progression for the school.

Work with the dancers:

The two Indian dancers spent the first two workshops teaching the children basic movements, particularly of their hands and feet. The emphasis was on encouraging the children to express themselves in a controlled and clear way. There was a lot of physical contact between the children and the dancers as they were helped to adopt the traditional positions. The musicians who, on one occasion, accompanied the dancers also contributed to the life of the school. Although they spoke little English, they strongly impressed the children with their interest in them and their professionalism as musicians.

Comment

Indian classical dance demands control and thought as well as feeling. This proves to be very good for children with learning difficulties. There seems to be a relationship between physical and academic sequencing.

Future work

It is hoped that the two Indian dancers will visit the school once a term to work with the children on various curriculum areas, the first based on the river that flows through the village, and its influence on the life of the community.

The school has involved the community in all its work and sought to make clear the multicultural dimensions. Some of the finance for the dance workshops came from a village fund.

8 Cowboy Christmas
An alternative Christmas play

Background

An urban junior school with 250 on roll. The production/performance invoived most of them.

Aims: to develop the following Concepts, Skills and Attitudes:

- to promote the idea of a spiritual dimension to life

- to raise awareness of:

  the inside/outside issue
  the conflict between good and bad

- to develop good relationships and co-operation

- to develop self-expression through drama and music

- to encourage:

  empathy for outsiders
  a personal set of values by which children can live their lives

  growing sensitivity — so that attitudes may change in the light of fresh knowledge

Process

1. A fresh look at the Nativity

The idea behind the play was to give the children and the audience a contrast to the Christmas story, something totally different. One teacher wrote the music, another the lyrics. The children developed the story from a skeleton idea. Some children played characters, some sang in the choir and others played musical instruments.

2. The story

The play opens with a saloon in 'Greengate Gulch'. All the townspeople, including the sheriff and his deputies, are there, singing dancing and drinking at Sal's bar. The doors open and Jo and Maria, two outsiders, enter. There's a sudden hush. Everyone looks at the two newcomers.But when they ask for accommodation, everyone ignores them. The sheriff and his three deputies (unknown to the townsfolks), are cattle rustlers. They lay the blame for their deeds upon any outsider who happens to be in town. Visitors are falsely accused, then convicted by the townsfolk and sent to work as slaves in the gold mines.

Maria is pregnant and the only offer of help and friendship she receives is from Sal. As the time for her baby to be born is near, Sal allows Jo and Maria to sleep in her livery stable. She keeps the news secret because the town is so unfriendly to outsiders.

While Jo and Maria are resting quietly in a corner of the stable, they overhear the sheriff and his deputies plotting a cattle-rustling expedition. The blame is to fall on Jo and Maria. The.crime is

duly committed. Jo tells the townsfolk what he has overheard but no-one believes him because he is an outsider. So he and Maria are banished to the gold mines.

However, one of the deputies is the Marshal's sheriff in disguise. She is neither a man nor is she the sheriff's person, but has been sent to infiltrate the sheriff's gang and discover what is going on. Jo's story is just the evidence she needs. She arrests the sheriff and two deputies and takes them to prison.

Meanwhile, in the gold mines, the pregnant Maria gets help and support from the other slaves.

When they are set free, Jo and Maria return to Greengate Gulch. In the livery stable of the saloon, Maria gives birth to her baby.

To mark the birth, the scene in the stable darkens, along with the whole school hall. Chris de Burgh's record 'A Child is born' is heard. In pairs, the cast, the choir and the musicians enter the hall by a rear door, each carrying a lighted candle. Slowly, with reverence and wonder they greet the newly born baby. They stand round the crib, the light from their candles illuminating their faces.

Comment

One of the memorable and magic moments of the play was the intense feeling and spirituality created by the final scene. An invited audience of infant children sat spellbound and completely wrapped up in the moment.

The involvement, commitment and humour of all involved was obvious. There was much cohesion and ownership of the production because the children took on the skeleton idea; they made it their own and it grew from within.

It was interesting to watch how Saloon Sal grew in strength and effectiveness as she challenged the stereotype the townspeople held about outsiders.

Further work

1. The children could be asked to consider who the "outsiders" might be:

i) in their school

ii) in their town

iii) in their county

iv) in the country.

2. **Role play:**
The children invent a Jo and Maria scenario using the present day and their own town as the setting.

3. Having defined the "outsider" and the predicaments they often find themselves in, the children explore ways that they themselves could support outsiders in their struggle for equal rights.

9 A feeling in my bones

Background

A parochial Church of England primary school with 37 children on roll

Note:

For the last three years Cumbria has invited Theatre Centre to provide workshops and performances for teachers and children. The themes always explore issues such as inequality, racism, sexism and cultural identity.

In 1989 the content and themes of the play was particularly emotive for children in Cumbria. Below we give:

    i)   a synopsis

    ii) some of the themes, and

    iii) a unit designed to develop children's thinking.

A village school in Cumbria took all its junior children to see the play. Their follow-up work is described here.

---

i) *A Synopsis*

Over the Cumbrian Hillside walks a woman, a woman with a briefcase in one hand and a soggy map in the other. This visit signals a series of upheavals in the lives of three people.

Joyce has been sent by 'Lakeside Holidays' to buy up homes to be used as holiday houses. Trapped by a snowstorm, she begins to question the responsibility she carries. Sean, a ten year old boy, and his mother Emer, must in turn face the realities of eviction.

With unexpected help from Matt, a soldier from Roman times, and from Sean's granny, the characters make discoveries about unfamiliar places and an unknown past. Their story shows how such discoveries can influence our perceptions of ourselves, our culture and the world in which we live.

THEATRE CENTRE MIXED COMPANY

IN TRANSIT

---

ii) *"A Feeling in my bones"* — Themes

Identity
- Names
- Family histories
- Britain's ancient past
- Common roots

Change
- Progress
- Resistance
- Personal development
- Decisions
- Journeys
- Dispossession
- Roads

Ownership
- Privacy
- Secrets
- Buying & selling
- Power
- Money
- Land
- Territory

Responsibility
- Following orders
- Taking sides
- Action
- Deserting
- Being brave

Differences
- Fear & misunderstanding
- Town & country
- Strangers
- Prejudice
- Race

---

iii) *Sean*

Sean is faced with a series of decisions during the play. Each time he makes a decision he has to choose what action to take. Ask the class to complete the questions below as if they were Sean making a decision:

- *Shall I join in calling the Snailman names, or shall I...?*
- *Shall I throw a stone at the Snailman, or shall I...?*

- *Shall I tell Mum about Matt, or shall I...?*
- *Shall I lie to Joyce about Granny, or shall I...?*

Ask them to make up similar questions to show the choices he might be considering at the end of the play.

- *Are some of these choices more difficult than others?*
- *What are the feelings or events that might lead him to take one course of action over another?*
- *Which courses of action might be useful or 'right'?*
- *Can you think of any other situations when people have had to make difficult choices about what action to take?*

Developments

It might be useful to focus on the consequences of certain actions by asking the class to write a news article or letter describing what happens after Sean and Emer have left their home.

1. Brainstorming: urban-rural life

The children, in groups of four, chose words to express their positive and negative feelings about:-

i) village

ii) town

iii) city

On large sheets of paper, each group made a web of the words. The children's ideas included: (see above).

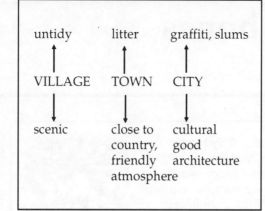

untidy	litter	graffiti, slums
↑	↑	↑
VILLAGE	TOWN	CITY
↓	↓	↓
scenic	close to country, friendly atmosphere	cultural good architecture

2. Moving house

Using their own experiences about moving house, the children explored their feelings.

3. Role play of Sean's situation

The children imagined that they were being forced out of their homes by property developers. They presented their role plays. The children thought about:-

i)   the Sean figure's feelings

ii) the property developer's feelings.

4. Newspaper article

The children became reporters and wrote a follow-up story about either the redevelopment of the property or about how Sean was getting on in his new home. An example is shown on the right.

5. Poems: Feelings

The children were invited to chose an emotion and express it in a poem. Most of the children were influenced by Sean's strong character and identified closely with his feelings of loneliness and frustration. Others wrote about happiness and excitement, again in relation to Sean. Opposite on page 27 are two examples.

THEY'VE RUINED MY HOME

Sean O'Farrell and his mother Emer lived in an old house in Cumbria. The Lakeside holidays thought that it was the right house for them to change it into a holiday home. The O'Farrells did not own the house so they could not decide to sell or not sell.

The house needed alot of alterations but they started right away. They put double glazing in and Central heating. Sean and Emer had to go and live in Manchester with Sean's Auntie. It was a big change of lifestyle for them both. The lakeside people say "They will get used it" That's there views

House now

Interview on Sean

"Are you happy with all the alterations which they've done to your Old house?"
"Well, no I am not very happy with the changes, as it has changed the countryside around the house."
"I can see you are not very pleased with the changes but would you come back and stay for 1 week?"
"No I don't think I could because they have ruined my life."
Reporter Kerry Whalley

Loneliness

I feel lonley and rejected,
My skin is a different colour.
People stare and point, laugh and joke,
They talk amongst them selves,
But they talk differently,
I wish I was like them.

Corrin

6. Simulation: closer to home

The council planned to build a main road through Scales village, which would entail demolishing six houses. The children identified the houses on a map.

The children took roles as:

i) the occupants of the houses under threat

ii) other villagers

iii) council members

iv) commuters who did not live in the village but who used the road to get to work in Barrow.

Those in role of the occupants of the six houses decided to form an action committee and petitioned the rest of the villagers to support their cause.

At an open meeting, very forceful views were expressed, although there was no resolution, only a date set for another meeting.

Frustration

When You are Frustrated
You don't know what to do
You wish You could   do
Something
But everything You try
Seems a waste of time.
Everything comes out Without
success.
Oh what a mess
You sit in a little corner
and wish all Your life would
go away.
Thats how Frustration is.
You get it every day.

Out of role, the children discussed their feelings. The council members knew that they could have 'bulldozed on ahead' but had not exercised that power at the meeting. A few children said that they would not have wanted to be councillors. They pointed out the dilemma of sympathising with the villagers on the one hand and, on the other, recognition that the road would have to go through someone else's village if not through Scales.

Resources

Theatre Centre, Hanover School, Noel Road, London NW 8BD.

For large scale maps and plans of proposed roads and housing developments contact your local planning office.

Ten primary and two secondary schools in West Cumbria took part in this project, some involving all the classes, others choosing one or two classes. This article describes how some schools chose to explore *The Worlds in our County*

Aims: to develop the following Concepts, Skills and Attitudes:

- an appreciation of the diversity of people, experience and lifestyles in a seemingly 'white' part of the world.

- an appreciation of the fact that people from many racial, ethnic and cultural groups have important roles in the community.

- using local source material to learn about the presence and influence of, for example, black people in Cumbria over the centuries

- empathy for people treated as 'outsiders'

- understanding how racism and other inequalities are forms of injustice

Background

In September 1988, schools in West Cumbria were invited to take part in **Worlds In Our County.** Each participating school received a booklet, produced by group of five teachers, which offered the following ideas and information:

1. The Concepts, Skills and Attitudes set out in Cumbria's **Curriculum Paper Number 14** can all become part of the curriculum and school ethos and can all be explored in the context of the immediate community. (see chart in Introduction page 4)

2. The multicultural dimension may enrich activities already planned in the schools.

3. Children's work will form part of an exhibition at Whitehaven Museum in April 1989.

4. The Curriculum Development Officer for Multicultural Education and the Arts in Education Officer have a small amount of money available and can help with planning classroom activities, resources, workshops with professional artists.

5. Local industry and Northern Arts are supporting the Project.

6. Some topic webs produced by local teachers are included, suggesting how themes such as language, the movement of people, work, names... can be a focus for developing the concepts, skills and attitudes in the context of the local community.

CUMBRIANS
Who are they?

Factory workers, fishermen, farmers, teachers, home workers, off-comers, working class, middle class, Poles, Latvians, Scots, Irish, Welsh, Chinese, Indians, Jews, Hindus, Christians, atheists, tall, short, fat, thin, black, white, rural, urban, travellers from other lands.

CUMBRIA

The Worlds in Our County

An exhibition of work by West Cumbrian Children on
"The Worlds in Our County"
at Whitehaven Museum
April 19th – 28th, 1989

ARTS IN EDUCATION
For West Cumbria

What the schools did... some ideas, processes, activities, research...

'Kindercot' School

A small nursery school, all white, serving largely working class community.

The children carefully compared themselves with one another to find out what made them the same or different from each other. They also considered the differences in their lifestyles. A very useful resource for this approach is: *Myself, I'm Special* from ACER

The children's work on the project was displayed with the accompanying notes reprinted here.

MYSELF

LOOKING AT SIMILARITIES AND DIFFERENCE

The children, aged three and four years, have been looking at themselves and other children, making comparisons and looking at differences and similarities.

They started off by looking in mirrors and making drawings of themselves. They examined eye and hair colours, height, size of hands and feet, gender, different types of families, different areas they lived in.

They examined the senses and discovered more similarities. They paid particular attention to smell, touch and taste.

They compared their drawings, paintings, computer work, woodwork and pottery. Blindfolded, they handled specimens of stones, twigs and leaves, and categorised them as rough or smooth. They examined fruit and vegetables for taste and smell.

Our Hair
The wheel showed the variety of length, texture, colour...

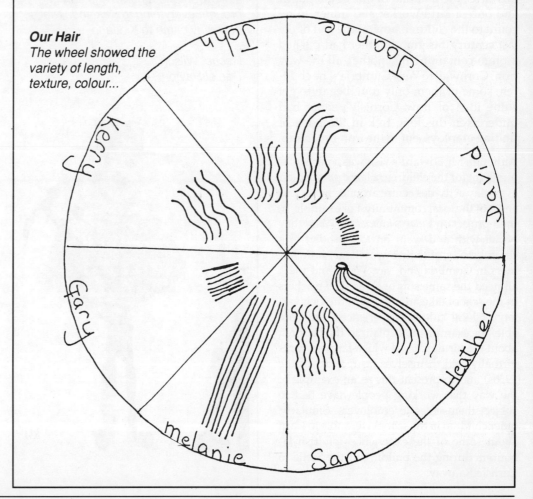

'Villager' School

A village school with 37 children. The local community is made up of long established farming families, a small number of people related to a once thriving iron-ore mining community and an increasing number of 'off-comer' families [usually well off professional people, often with no family links with the area].

The teacher of the Infants class wanted to bring to life for the children the experiences of the local community. She invited Mr Edwards, the grandad of one of the pupils and once a farm worker and miner, to recount to the children how, at the end of the last century, his grandmother had pushed a pram containing his mother, all the way from Cornwall to West Cumbria. The children, some of them only four, began to get some idea of how Cornish people had undertaken this long trek in the hope of finding employment in the iron-ore mines.

Although Mr Edward's visit was a particular highlight for the children, a large part of their everyday activities centre around the experiences of the local community. For example, in their project on *Villages around the World* they began with and went on to consider, in a careful study of their own village, how farmers in Cumbria and, say, Wales and India all need the same sort of skills. The teachers in the school take an interest in the rich variety of local cultural experiences. They are able, for example, to explain to the children about the hiring fairs at which farm servants virtually sold themselves (as recently as the 1950s) and to present this as an example of the way that working people have had to subject themselves to employers. Similarly, older children in the school were able to learn about some of the experiences of Irish labourers during the building of the Settle to Carlisle Railway.

The Tin Miners Come To Kirkland

When the iron ore mines opened in Kirkland they needed men to work in the mines. In Cornwall the tine mines closed down and the men had no jobs and no money so they left Cornwall. Lots of them walked all the way to Kirkland. They looked for a job in the new mines. Then their families came on a train with the furniture and the children with them. The train stopped at Rowrah and a horse and cart brought everything to Kirkland. That's how they came to Kirkland.

Rachel Wilson
Daniel Hayton

Settle to Carlisle Railway.

They started to make a railway from Settle to Carlisle which is 72 miles in 1869 which is about 120 years from now.
It took 3,000 navvies (navigators) to make the railway.
Settle to Carlisle is the roughest Country in Britain.
They built the railway over the fells to Appleby.
They thought it would take four years but they were wrong because it took about seven years.
They had to work in all weathers and when it was windy they were blown off viaducts.
When it was winter it was really freezing but they still had to work.
The diseases they caught were Smallpox and Cholera and they were spread quite easily and many people were killed.
Four hundred navvies were killed in the first twenty miles.
There are many navvies buried in St. Leonards and Chapel.
People came to build the railway from nearby and a long way away. The shanty towns they built were called Sebastapool, Battywide Hoe and Inkerman. They were only made of metal and wood so they didn't keep the navvies very warm.

'Highcliff' School

This primary school sits on a cliff-top overlooking Whitehaven. Although many people know of Whitehaven's importance in the eighteenth century trade with the 'new world', few realise that black people, originating from countries in Africa, have been part of the community for centuries. The curator of the local museum provided information on this from churches in town and the older children used a world map to learn about some of the many connections Whitehaven had with the world.

Young children researched their own families finding out why grandparents and parents had come to the area.

My grandfather
My grandfather came from Scotland. He came for work eventually he got work in a slaughter house. He became the head of the slaughter house. He left 2 or 3 years later. He now works at Robert Jacksons and Son

PLACES CONNECTED BY SEA WITH WHITEHAVEN TWO HUNDRED YEARS AGO

1. WHITEHAVEN
2. BLACK RIVER, JAMAICA; NIGRA HILL BAY, JAMAICA
3. BRAZIL
4. SLIGO
5. QUEBEC
6. WEXFORD
7. BOMBAY
8. DOMINICA
9. LANDS END
10. BONNY
11. MADEIRA
12. PORT A PRINCE, ST. DOMINGO
13. CHARLESTOWN, SOUTH CAROLINA
14. RIGA
15. BELFAST
16. EDINBURGH
17. ANTIGUA
18. NORFOLK, VIRGINIA
19. NEW YORK
20. ANGOLA
21. COAST OF GUINEA
22. GRENADA
23. BRISTOL
24. MARTINIQUE

The names of all these places were found on gravestones in St. Nicholas churchyard by class seven.

There were sailors from Whitehaven who died from disease or were shipwrecked and drowned at each one of these places, between 1760 and 1830.

Records of the births, deaths and marriages of black and mulatto people in Whitehaven in the eighteenth and nineteenth centuries.

*Mulatto, as referred to in the list below, probably meant people of both black and white parentage.

HOLY TRINITY REGISTER

marriages — None

ST. JAMES REGISTERS

1758 Sep 7 Thomas Whitehaven, a negro of ripe years, baptised

1766 Aug 6 Peter Geoffrey, a mulatto of ripe years

1769 Feb 25 Peter Thompson, a negro of ripe years

1777 Dec 28 Phebe Jackson, an adult negro

1780 Nov 25 Michael of Robert Collins, a mulatto

1798 Nov 11 Mary Christian Grasett, a mulatto aged 12

ST. BEES REGISTER

Baptised in Whitehaven

1700 Jan 7 Jane, a negro servant of Mr George Gale

S.N.R. Marriages

Dec 23 Paul Jones, a negro and Susannah Jones, a negro, by T.M. witness William Young

S.N.R. Births or Baptisms

1774 Mar 12 Archibald Marshall, a black man

1776 Sep 16 William Sampson, a black man

Thomas Caton, a black man

Paul Jones, a black man

Susannah Jones, a black woman

Sep 17 John Wilson, a black man

Sep 21 Francis Oates, a black man

Edna Oates, a black woman

Jonas, of Francis and Edna Oates, a black boy

1776 Sep 21 Samuel of same, a black boy

John Richards, a black man

Susannah Faddy, a black woman

Charlotte, of Susannah Faddy, a black child

Jenny Warwick, a black woman

Dec 10 Richard Bush, a black man

1777 April 23 Thomas Harrison, a black boy

Richard Hilton, a black man

Samuel Thompson, a black man

Sep 28 James Richards, a black man

1782 Jan 6 Isaac Dharriett, a black man or mulatto

Mary Dharriett, a black woman

James Bannister, a black man

Sep 1 John Damond, a black man

Anthony Flann, a black man

1784 May 9 Richard Catterick, a black man

1785 April 1 Peter Mordas, a black man

1791 Oct 9 Cyta Harrington, a black man

1794 June 2 John Barnes, a black man

1795 Oct 27 John Paterson, a black man

1796 Nov 6 William Johnson, a black boy

ST. NICHOLAS CHURCH, WHITEHAVEN

1762 Jan 22 John McLoy, a black man

1766 May 28 Othello of John Hartley, a black man

1773 Oct 9 Daniel Dixon, a black man

1779 Oct 29 Jenny Warwick, a black woman

1785 Feb 7 Isaac Dharriett, a mulatto

1795 Aug 29 Betty Day, a black girl

1802 May 4 Solomon Sentforth, a black man

'Hill Fort' School

The teacher of the ten year olds in a primary school in a small market town, regarded them as a particularly sensitive and alert class, and she was confirmed in this when working with them on **Worlds in Our County.** They researched the situation of evacuees during the second world war, using local newspapers, interviews with ancillary workers in the school and others in the community to build up a picture of how it felt for the young evacuees, arriving from Newcastle-upon-Tyne during the first week of the war. They acted out a play about war-time dislocations and how these can highlight issues such as class. As well as their concern about evacuees, the children also showed deep concern about the racism experienced by black people and what this might be like for a black person in a 'white' world. As a part of their investigation into the experiences of people who are regarded as outsiders, they invited a local Jewish person into school (this is described on page 78).

There is a wealth of evidence in west Cumbria which reflects the diversity of the population for example:

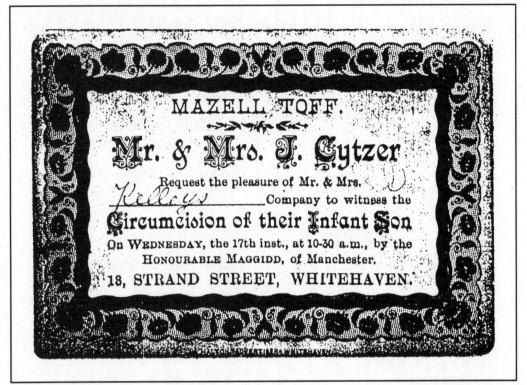

MAZELL TOFF.

Mr. & Mrs. J. Cytzer

Request the pleasure of Mr. & Mrs.

_Kellcys_____ Company to witness the

Circumcision of their Infant Son

On WEDNESDAY, the 17th inst., at 10-30 a.m., by the HONOURABLE MAGGIDD, of Manchester.

18, STRAND STREET, WHITEHAVEN.

Material supplied by Russell Sellick
Whitehaven Civic Society

Jews

I dread to think what they'd do,
If they found me or you.
They'd take us to one of those camps,
It would be all smelly dark and damp.
They'd take our clothes they wouldn't feed us.
Oh please, please help us.

Louise Ratcliffe

From: 'Local Intelligence' 16 July 1850.

Mr. R.C. Hildyard, the member for this borough, voted in the minority in favour of going into committee on the Home-made Spirits In Bond Bill. The Hon. Gentleman on Tuesday evening presented petitions from various parts of Cumberland against the admission of Jews in Parliament.

'Dale' School

In this junior school, the project centred around imaginative work on the theme of 'insiders, outsiders'.

<u>Belonging</u>

belonging is a good thing

because you belong some where

And you have good fellings.

you can tell if a person

belongs some where by the looks

in there eyes,

when you belong some were you fell

welcome

when you see other people make

Them very welcome

but I think I belong in

whitehaven with all my frends

to keep them some cumpornay

and to have a good

sense of humur.

in whitehaven its a free place

but if you move you'll be lonky

and miss the freedom

so if you see any

one who needs help,

help them because you will

be in that way some day

10 year old

Corinna's picture tried to explain some of her ideas about black people and white people as insiders or outsiders.

The peripatetic teacher with responsibility for supporting children with English as a Second Language began a language survey and, within a very small geographical area which at first glance appears to be entirely homogeneous, discovered:

> **Some of the Languages spoken in West Cumbria:**
> Urdu
> Punjabi
> Cantonese
> Polish
> Italian
> French
> French Creole
> Danish

'Seacliffe' School

Every class in one junior school researched the origins of their families. They discovered that their parents and grandparents had lived all over Cumbria, Britain and the world. The graphs they designed which showed, for example, the birthplaces of parents and grandparents, demonstrated clearly that there was a wealth of experience within the school community. It's interesting to speculate that moves from rural parts of Cumbria to the industialised coast may have been almost as great a cultural upheaval as moves between continents.

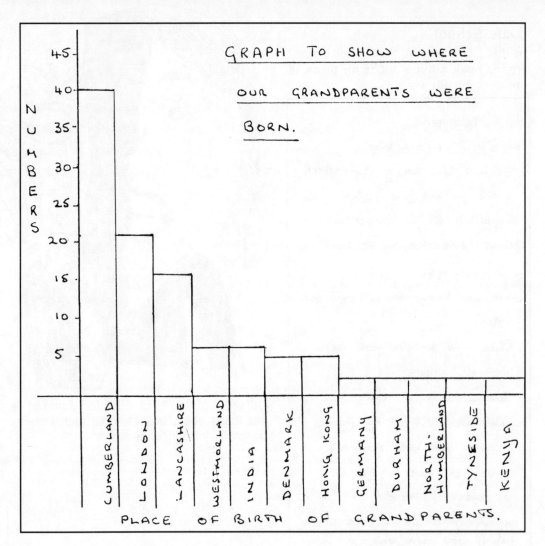

Section III:
THE WAY WE FEEL

This section deals with children discussing their feelings about themselves, the people around them and the world outside. By creating a space to work on issues such as differences and similarities and injustice, we hope to begin a process which will encourage children to participate in school and in the wider community as confident and questioning individuals.

11 Feelings

Background:
A village primary school with 183 on roll, a class of 10 and 11 year olds.

AIMS: to develop the following Concepts, Skills and Attitudes:

- deepening chidren's awareness of their own feelings and what it means to be an individual with one's own feelings and emotions.

- developing skills of cooperation, negotiation and communication

- expressing their feelings in a variety of ways

- relating to each other through work and play

- supporting one another by valuing the contributions that each can make

- valuing themselves as individuals

Process.

1. **Happy & sad feelings**
The pupils sat in a circle. Each child was given two flash cards, one of the happy and one of the sad face. They talked about their pictures for a few minutes and agreed that the faces were indeed happy and sad.

The children were asked to respond to a set of questions without talking but using only their flash card.

These were the questions to which they were to respond:

- How do you feel if someone pushes you?

- How do you feel when someone grins at you?

- How do you feel when you're asked to read aloud in class?

- How do you feel when a friend is ill?

- How do you feel when someone tells you that they like you?

- How do you feel if it rains all day?

- How do you feel when you're on holiday?

- How do you feel in the dark?

- How do you feel if a stranger offers you a lift?

- How do you feel when someone gives you a present?

(Questions adapted from: **Self-Esteem: a classroom affair; 101 ways to help children like themselves** (see Resources).

Some children answered certain questions by showing both flash cards. The teacher paid particular attention to such replies, for instance:

Teacher: How do you feel about reading aloud?

Child: I may be worried about reading aloud in case I make a mistake, but I am happy at being asked and happy when I've done it.

2. Sharing feelings

Still in a circle, the children shared their feelings by completing the following sentences — this time, verbally.

- Talking in front of the class makes me feel...

- When I make things with my hands I feel...

- When reading to the class I feel...

- When I arrive at school each morning, I feel...

- Giving a one minute talk on a topic, I feel...

- When I share my sweets I feel...

- During playtime I feel...

- Friends make me feel...

- When I have to tidy a classroom, I feel...

(Questions adapted from: **Self-Esteen: A Classroom Affair 101 ways to help children like themselves.**)

Other sets of sentences for completion could be about home life, holidays etc.

The activity was run rather like a 'brainstorm' session, the teacher going round the circle and beginning each sentence in front of a child, to which that child responded spontaneously.

3. A feelings brainstorm

Using a system of random numbering (see work on small groups), the children were divided into groups of five. Each group had a piece of sugar paper and a felt-tip pen, and appointed a scribe and spokesperson. Under a large heading, FEELINGS, each group wrote down as many things as they could in four or five minutes.

Some of their responses were:

---

big small scared great helpful angry bad worried small good kind f at miserable coward bully stupid sad stupid excited conned cute naughty lonely nerd ungrateful mad uncomfortable horrible dignified cooperative concerned helpless

FEELINGS

empty neglected shocked surprised idiotic radical fretting bonkers fuming upset caring mental embarassed shy friendly unliked exhausted happy funny rude clam cool disappointed free playful enlightened stupid horrid helpful disgusted

---

Each spokesperson then shared their group's answer with the whole class

4. Definition of feelings

The groups were asked to write their definition of feelings.

The teacher suggested that they might begin their answer under the heading: Feelings are...

The children were asked to choose another spokesperson who then shared their group's replies with the rest of the class.

Children's replies:

- *Feelings are something that are inside you and sometimes hurt you.*

- *Feelings are important to people and is a way of communicating.*

- *Feelings are what you feel inside you*

- *Feelings are thoughts. Feelings are things inside you. Things in your brain. They can drive you crazy. They can drive you into dangerous things.*

- *Feelings are something that are inside you that can be harmful or unharmful.*

5. Masks

A new representative for each group collected one of a series of mask-like faces from the teacher.

The masks were all different; there were more masks than there were groups; they were placed face down so that the child could not see which face s/he was choosing.

Above: Masks used by the children for the tableaux activity.
[Masks adapted from: **Self-Esteem; a classroom affair**]

Each group spent a few minutes looking at their mask and had to agree what feeling(s) it conveyed. Their next task, for which they had about 10 minutes, was to work out a tableau to show the rest of the class the feeling(s) their face masks portrayed.

The groups then presented their tableaux. The idea was that they should 'freeze' at the moment they felt they were portraying the mask. They held this pose for about 30 seconds, after which the class could ask questions, as they tried to guess what feelings the tableau had shown.

6.   Visualisation

The teacher then asked the children to find their own space and lie down comfortably; to close their eyes and breathe deeply and gently. She helped those who needed to relax by placing a soothing hand on head or back. After a couple of minutes for the children to settle, the teacher read the poem: *The Loner* (see Resources). She read it through twice, presenting it as an example of one person's feelings.

Whilst the children were still relaxed, the teacher asked them to think about their own feelings along the following lines:

- Choose a situation that you are willing to share. How did you feel?

- What could you say about your feelings?

- How might you want to express them?

- What other ways might you want to express them?

The children were given a short time to reflect on the questions.

7.   Discussion of children's experiences
The teacher allowed sufficient time to follow up issues raised by the children.

Further Work

In addition to expressing their feelings verbally, the children can be offered:

paint, pencils, crayons, felt-tips, paper, wool, materials etc., to allow them to express themselves in any way they wish.

Resources:

Self-Esteem a classroom affair: 101 ways to help children like themselves by Michele and Craig Borba. Harper & Row.

The Loner: Card AO2.4 by Julie Holden. Philip Green.

Who Listens?

12

Background:

A rural primary school with 201 on roll. Twenty-two ten and eleven year olds were involved in this project.

This work followed on from the work on Feelings (see Chapter 12) but formed a separate unit.

AIMS: to develop the following Concepts, Skills and Attitudes:

- empathy
- communication and listening skills
- a sense of fairness and justice
- an awareness of inequality in society

Process:

1. **Sharing an injustice.**
   i) The children sat in pairs facing each other. Each had a turn in which to describe an experience of injustice and say how they felt about it. The teacher chose not to listen.

   ii) After several minutes, the children formed groups of six, where each child introduced their partner, and went on to tell the group what had happened to her/him and how s/he had felt.

   iii) In the whole group discussion that followed, the children said how important it was that people listened to them. Many said that they felt angry and hurt when no-one listened.

2. **Listening to others**
   With the children still in their sixes, the teacher introduced the idea of:

   groups of people in their village, their county, in Britain, in the world to whom society does not listen.

   She asked:

   Which groups of people in society might feel that no-one listens to them?

   The children suggested the following:

   > *old people, children, poor people, single people such as widows, single parents, lepers, beggars, criminals, Greenpeace, people with disabilities like deafness or in wheelchairs, prostitutes, sick people, tramps, foreigners, drug addicts, drunks, workers like bus drivers, small parties in politics, coaches and referees, policemen.*

   The teacher accepted these views of the children without comment.

3. **What might they say?**
   Still in their small groups, the children:
   i) discussed the list on the board
   ii) chose one of the categories listed and explored the question:

   What might these groups say to us if we sat down and listened to them?

   Opposite are some of their answers:

4. **Not now Bernard!**
   The teacher read the story: *Not Now Bernard* to the children. The she asked them to role-play in their groups.

   How could the boy in the story get his parents to listen?

   Bernard could, for example:
   - tickle his mother;
   - scream and stamp;
   - shout, 'Nobody ever listens to me'
   - switch off the electricity;
   - take hold of his dad's hands and say, 'Listen to *me* now.'
   - say, 'You're always telling me to listen to you. Now it's fair for you to listen to me.'

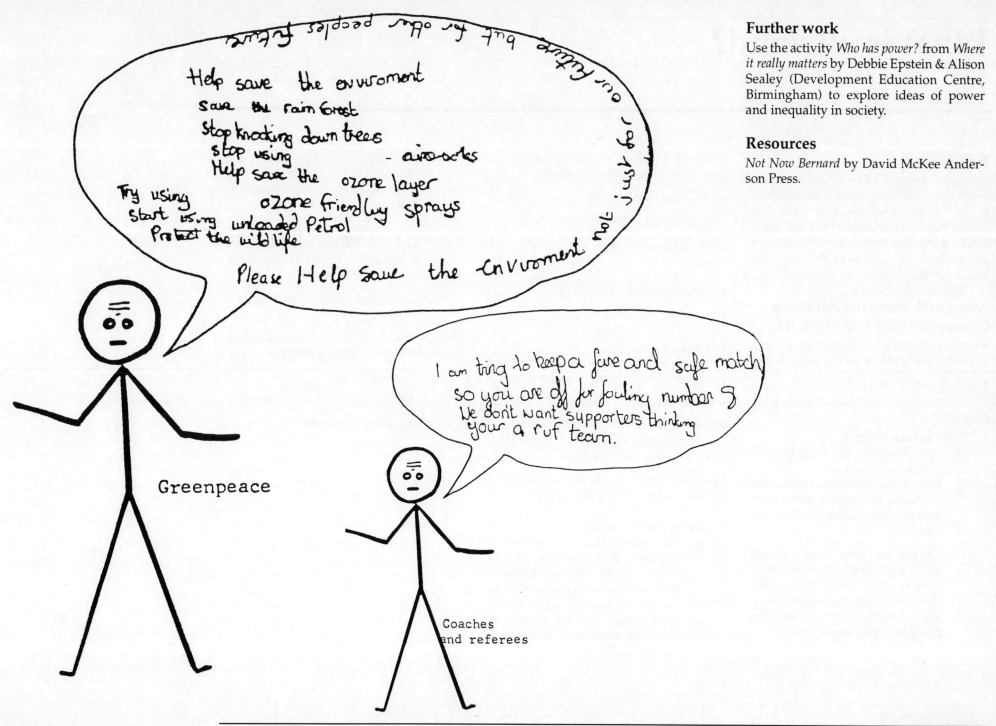

Further work

Use the activity *Who has power?* from *Where it really matters* by Debbie Epstein & Alison Sealey (Development Education Centre, Birmingham) to explore ideas of power and inequality in society.

Resources

Not Now Bernard by David McKee Anderson Press.

What is a friend?

13

Background

This topic was tackled by a class of six and seven year olds (early in the Autumn term) in an Infant/Nursery school. The class looked at friendship as part of an R.E. topic which also included other curriculum areas, especially language development and the communication of abstract ideas.

Aims: to develop the following Concepts, Skills and Attitudes:

- understanding and accepting similarities and differences in people

- valuing other people

Process:

1. **What makes a friend?**
   i) The children talked about who their friends were.
   Friends will include pets and possibly even toys, for example teddy bears, especially for children who have few friends.

   ii) The teacher asked *'Why do you like your friend?'* and listed the children's answers. Based on their list, she presented the qualities necessary for friendship. The children discussed these ideas.

The teacher then asked: *"What makes a good friend?"* and the children replied:

- *Someone who loves you*

- *Someone who cares for you*

- *Someone who shares their sweets with you*

- *Someone who plays with you*

- *Someone who listens to you*

2. **A friend is...**
The teacher gave out white silhouettes of people and the children wrote on them:

A friend is...

Those who could, wrote several sentences, but every child contributed something, some with the teacher's help.

The silhouettes made an eyecatching mobile, a celebration of friendship.

3. Further developments
   i) The children then chose a sheet of coloured paper and drew on it an outline figure. The paper was of different sizes as well as colours, so the result was tall figures, and short, gangly and fat, some with long arms and some with short... a variety of odd shapes.

   ii) the children saw that though the silhouettes had similarities — a head, two legs — they were also different.

   iii) The children's silhouettes were made into a frieze with the figures holding hands. Those of the same colour were kept apart.

   iv) The teacher asked: *In what ways are the figures different?*

Then she asked whether the differnces they had identified would be found in:

   the class?

   the school?

   any group of people?

Comment:

The topic was particularly appropriate for this class because certain children stood out. There was for example, a leukemia sufferer who had lost his hair during treatment and was called 'Baldy' when he came back to school, and another child whom no one played with.

Certain stories could take the work forward:

Tusk, Tusk by McKee, D. Anderson 1978

The Elephant with Rosy Coloured Ears by Barbara Resch, Black. 1973.

Mr & Mrs Hay The Horse by Janet Ahlberg Viking/Kestrel 1981.

The children could be helped to observe each other's behaviour, working in small groups. They could, for example, look at:

Who plays with whom?

What sort of games do they play?

Are they using playground equipment?

Are some of the children with an adult?

At a later stage children may discuss:

- how conflicts arise
- ways of solving them

Future Work

So 'friendship' should be kept on the agenda and the children constantly reminded of their comments and encouraged to apply them in resolving problems about their own relationships.

Resources

World Studies Handbook 8-13. David Hicks & Simon Fisher, Oliver & Boyd

Everybody's Special

14

Background:

Four and five year olds (20-30 in each group) in an infant school on a council housing estate in a coastal town, worked on this project.

Aims: to develop the following concepts, skills:

- positive self-image
- cooperation
- communication
- some understanding of similarities and differences

Process:

Reason for Action

The teacher in charge of the reception unit was concerned at the increasing levels of aggression amongst the children. She felt that this came in part from poor self-esteem and the local community's possible feelings that it is not highly valued. She decided to plan a set of activities to help the children feel positively about themselves and each other. Each session lasted about 25 minutes.

Session One:

1. Song: *Come on Boys and Girls*
This song is designed to mention every child's name so that each can feel important. [It was used at the beginning of every session.]

2. Experiencing Stillness
The children closed their eyes while the teacher very quietly counted to five, almost under her breath.

3. Rainstorm
The teacher, as the conductor of the storm, stood in the middle of the circle. As with an orchestra, she brought each person into the storm (symphony) in turn. Standing in front of one person, she rubbed her hands together and the person imitated her, then turned to the next 'player', until she had brought everyone in the circle into the action. Then, while everyone was still rubbing hands together, the teacher came round to the first child again and started snapping her fingers. This motion also went around the circle, with each person continuing a motion until they had new directions from the conductor. The game went on to hands slapping thighs, and finally to slapping thighs and at the same time stamping feet — the crescendo of the storm. As with a thunder shower, the volume decreased as the conductor reversed the order of the movements around the circle, until the last person rubbing hands was silent.

Session Two:

1. Song

2. Experiencing Stillness

3. Magic Spot Name Game:
At this session there was a visitor who didn't know the children's names. They sat in a circle and the visitor explained that there was a magic spot right in the middle of the circle and that it was the special place where each child could stand to say her/his name. Gary confidently occupied the space and proudly proclaimed his name, as did most of the other boys. The girls edged diffidently towards the magic spot and whispered their names, except for Charlotte and Karon who were rather bolder.

4. The Same and Different
In pairs, the children watched as two adults demonstrated *The Same and Different*:

> Starting from the tops of our heads:
> Our hair is the same
> Our eyes are different
> My nose turns up and yours is straight
> Our skin is the same
> Our clothes are different
> ... and so on

Each pair of children found similarities and differences. (It helped to have a lot of adult helpers here!)

Emma

I let people play with my toys.

Session Three:

1. **Song**

2. **Experiencing Stillness**

3. **Everybody's Special**

The children sat in a large circle. Each child stood up in turn and the other children spent a few moments finding positive things to say about her, for example:

> Janine's got a nice smile.

> Timmy's hair is a lovely colour.

> I like Michaela's dress.

The child then chose one thing that had been said about her or suggested one of her own. The teacher wrote this in large letters at the bottom of a sheet of paper. Later the child drew a picture of him or herself emphasising the chosen feature and perhaps copying or tracing the words.

Session Four:

1. **Song**

2. **Experiencing Stillness**

3. **Parachute Game:**

The children all held onto the edges of a full size parachute spread out on the floor of the hall. By working together, they could make it billow up to make a huge green silk dome under which two or three children could play. Building on *Same and Different*, the children were asked to run through the 'tent' to change places with, for example someone with different colour eyes or the same colour hair.

4. **Meditation Dance:** (see Resources)

i. The children listened to the music while walking quietly around.

ii. They practised the dance steps:

Step slowly onto right foot

Then onto left foot

Then onto right foot

Sway back onto left foot

Repeat

iii. Each child made up his/her own words based on the previous session, for example,

> *I like my smile*

iv. The music, the steps and the words were put together.

This can be danced in a circle with each person placing their right hand on the left shoulder of the person in front of them.

Five year old Alison, who had never before joined in group work, participated fully — much to the teacher's delight.

Resources

Dancing games for children of all ages by Esther L. Nelson, Sterling Publ. Co. Oak Tree Publ Co.

The Friendly classroom for a small planet by Priscilla Prutzman, Avery Publ. Group Inc. Wayne, New Jersey (available from Friends' Book Centre, Friends' House, Euston Road, London NW1 2BJ).

SECTION IV:
DIFFERENT AND THE SAME

This section describes attempts to help children to appreciate, value and cooperate with people who may appear different, rather than to allow differences to divide and separate. If children can talk openly about the differences between people and groups, they may be able to recognise how those differences can be associated with inequality and then to consider ways of challenging some of the behaviour which can lead to injustice.

The Rainbow People 1

Background:
A Church of England Nursery/Infant school with an urban/rural catchment area.

Aims: to develop the following Concepts, Skills and Attitudes:
- to consider how people can be different
- to understand that although other people's beliefs, lifestyles, colour and language may be different, everyone has the same basic needs
- to imagine what it is like to be different from other groups of people
- to communicate through drama and discussion
- to cooperate with each other
- to value the contributions that each person can make
- to recognise other people's abilities and knowledge and think of ways that we can learn from them

- to value their own worth as individuals
- to appreciate the worth of our own and other groups' social, cultural and family background.

Process
1. The story of the 'Rainbow people' was part of a whole school topic on Colour.

The children did a lot of work on differences between individuals; eg. hair, eyes, skin, etc...

> We have different colour hair.
>
> And eyes.
>
> Sometimes their skin is a different colour.
>
> People talk differently
>
> Some people each different things
>
> I like eating Chinese food.

See story on page 46

A class of seven year olds discussed differences between people:

> My mummy has a friend who lives in another country. She talks a different way, but she is very nice.

The children talked about people they knew who spoke different languages or who spoke...

> the same as we do, but it sounds different.
>
> I know someone from Scotland...I can't understand him sometimes but he likes playing football with me.

The children enjoyed repeating some phrases in French, German and Japanese. One little boy was born in Japan and had lived there for three years.

A child asked him:

> Why don't you look Japanese if you were born there?

Christopher considered this and answered:

> I think it is because my mummy and daddy aren't.

2. The teacher told the story of the 'Rainbow People'. The children used it as a basis for dance and drama.

3. The children talked positively about people they knew and liked but who were different in some way.

4. The children discussed their reactions to situations or people who were different, saying that they usually laughed at them.

They considered what it was like to be laughed at.

The following are some questions that might help them explore this situation:

> Have you ever been laughed at because you're different?
>
> How does it feel to be laughed at?
>
> What did you want to do when you were laughed at?
>
> How can we help ourselves and each other when we are laughed at?

Note: As teachers, we will be sensitive to individual pupils' feelings. Discussion about differences apparent in the classroom won't always be appropriate. Sometimes it may be better to distance the issues by using stories, poems...(see resources).

Further Work:

1. Having given the children an opportunity to express their feelings about individuals and differences, a further step might be to explore which groups in society children can identify as being different. Then it may be possible to think about those groups who have less power than others and who suffer injustice.

2. This work may fit into a cross-curricular topic on colour.

For example:

National Curriculum Science

A.T.4 GENETICS AND EVOLUTION

i) differences and similarities between themselves e.g. hair/skin/eyes.

ii) different coloured skin or hair...compare parents hair colour with own hair.

A.T. 15 USING LIGHT & ELECTRO MAGNECTIC RADIATION

i) Prism — Rainbow breaking down light

Children's Comments

Children may make remarks about differences, unfairness, etc at any time. As teachers, we are sensitive to the value of these 'off the cuff' remarks. We may be able to capitalise on them.

For example, following up Christopher's explanation:

> *Why don't you look Japanese if you were born there?*
>
> *I think it's because my mummy and daddy aren't,*

the teacher might lead the children to further thought:

> Do we all look like our parents?
>
> Does where we are born affect how we look?
>
> Do Ethiopian/Japanese/French children look like their parents?
>
> Why do human beings look different from each other?

The Rainbow People

This is a condensed version of an original story *The Rainbow People* by Carolyn Askar (copyright).

In the beginning the world was very still and quiet. The ground seemed to be covered with dull coloured rocks and stones. If you took a closer look you could see that they were not stones, but tiny people who were not moving at all.

One day a wind blew over the land, which warmed the people and filled them with life and love. They began to move... to look at each other... to touch each other... to speak to each other... to care about each other.

As they explored their world, they found coloured ribbons lying on the ground. They were excited and ran about collecting them. Some chose blue, some red, some green, some yellow. They enjoyed tying the ribbons around each other and laughing at the bright colours.

Suddenly another wind blew. This time they shivered with cold. They looked at each other and realised they looked different... and they stopped trusting each other.

The reds gathered together and ran into a corner.

The blues gathered together and ran into a corner; the greens gathered together and ran into another corner. The yellows gathered together and ran into a corner.

They forgot that they had been friends and had cared for each other. The other colours just seemed different and strange. They built walls to separate themselves and keep the others out. But they found that:

The reds had water but no food.
(Mime feeling hungry)

The blues had food but no water.
(Mime feeling thirsty)

The greens had twigs to make fire but no shelter...
(Mime looking for shelter)

The yellows had shelter but nothing to keep them warm.
(Mime shivering with cold)

One day a stranger appeared and stood in the centre of the land. He looked in amazement at the people in their separate groups and said, 'Come on out everybody. What are you afraid of? Let's talk to each other!'.

The people peeped out at him, slowly and hesitantly they began to look around. The stranger said, 'Now just tell one another what you have got to give, and what you need to be given.'

The blues said 'We have plenty of food to give but we need water'. The reds said, 'We have plenty of water to give but we need food'. The greens said, 'We have plenty of wood for fire but we need shelter'. The yellows said, 'We have plenty of shelter but we need warmth.' The stranger said, 'Why don't you put together what you have and share it? Then you can all have enough to eat and drink, keep warm and have shelter'.

They talked and the feeling of love returned.

They remembered that they had been friends. They knocked down the walls and welcomed each other as old friends.

When they realised that the colours had divided them, they wanted to throw them away. But they knew that they would miss the richness of the bright colours. So instead they braided the colours to make a beautiful rainbow ribbon.

They called themselves the Rainbow People. The rainbow ribbon became their symbol of peace.

Instructions for Teacher

A narrator tells the story, with suitable pauses, while the children act out what is happening. Some words can be spoken by the children acting: You will need:

Brightly coloured streamers of crepe paper, ribbon or strips of material — blue, red, green and yellow. Allow more streamers than children so that the children can choose a colour. They start the play curled up very still on the ground.

Resources for further work

What is a family? Photopack. Development Education Centre Selly Oak College, Bristol Road, Birmingham.

Myself, I'm Special Afro-Carribean Education Resource Centre, Wyvil School, Wyvil Road, London SW8.

The Rainbow People 2

Background

A coastal village primary school with 250 on roll. A class of 10 - 11 year olds.

Aims: to develop the following Concepts, Skills and Attitudes:

- establishing that all human beings have the same basic needs

- understanding the concept of cooperation

- developing relationships with others

- understanding the role of the individual as a member of a group

- understanding the problems of interaction and communication between groups

- reaching a consensus as to what we all need to have an enjoyable life

- developing cooperation as an essential part of life

- developing self-expression and communication through speech, drama, friendship and creative activity

- developing an awareness of, and a readiness to respond to, the needs of others.

Process

1. The class was divided into groups of five. Each group was given a piece of paper and a thick felt-tip. On the top of their paper they wrote the following heading...

WHAT WE NEED FOR A GOOD LIFE

For five minutes the children brainstormed their ideas. The following emerged...

> family, friendship, shelter, food, warmth, health, help each other, power, love, sharing things, water, environment, care.

A spokesperson from each group reported their group's finding to the whole class. These were displayed. Sometimes pupils asked a group to elaborate their answer.

For example:

> What is the importance of the environment for a good life?
>
> *It provides us with scenery to relax in and to enjoy beauty and peace and quiet.*

The teacher then identified ideas that were common to all groups:

SHARING, CARING, COOPERATION

and these were discussed.

2. The children were asked to lie down and make themselves comfortable and relaxed. Once they were settled, the teacher told them the story of the Rainbow People (see p.46). Then she said they would be miming the story, and read it a second time so that they could remember the details.

3. Using crepe paper streamers in 4 colours, the class acted out the story. After the mime, the children made a large circle. They were asked what they thought was the message of the story and were given a minute's thinking time. Each child was able to contribute something to the feedback.

> Just because people look different you shouldn't reject them.
>
> Don't reject people just because they have different colours.
>
> It means everyone is different but you should be friendly no matter what colour you are.
>
> It means to be kind to one another and to help one another and to share things with each other.
>
> Look after each other and don't turn away from them if they look different.
>
> To care and look after people instead of leaving them out.
>
> I think it means everybody can be friends and work together.
>
> To be kind and share things. Don't just think about yourself.

4. Tribes

The children closed their eyes and the teacher placed a coloured sticky dot on the face of each child, where s/he could not see it. Only four colours were used as in the story. The children then opened their eyes and had to find the other members of their tribe without speaking.

To end the activity, the children told each other the ways in which they had managed to do this.

5. Donkey activity

Each group was given a set of donkey pictures. The story had been cut into six strips. The groups arranged them in a story.

The children either wrote or told each other what they thought was the message of the pictures.

(From: *The Donkey Story*)

6. Cooperative letters

Using only their bodies and the floor space, the children made human letters beginning with the letter x. It ended with the whole class down on the floor, making the word:

B R E A D

7. School Assembly

A whole school assembly was organised by the children, who narrated and mimed the story of the Rainbow People.

Resources:

The Rainbow People adapted from Caroline Askar. Christian Aid.

The Donkey Story. Quaker Peace Project. Friends Bookshop, Friends House, Euston Road, London NW1 2BJ.

Wilson — the Boy who wouldn't take off his blazer.

Background

A class of 24 five year olds in a nursery/infant Church of England Aided School.

Aims: to develop the following Concepts, Skills and Attitudes:

- a sense of belonging

- similarities and differences

- enter into the feelings of others

- explore feelings

Process

1. Starting with the Story

The teacher read *Long Blue Blazer*, the story of Wilson who comes to school for the first time and refuses to take off his blazer. When his mum arrives in a spaceship, Wilson finally takes off his blazer revealing a long blue tail! In the discussion that followed the reading, it was clear that the children had understood why Wilson had been so reluctant to remove his blazer and that they identified with his feelings. They considered what their reactions might have been if he had removed it earlier. The children also explored the idea that, inside, Wilson was the same as everyone else, experiencing the same feelings of pleasure and sadness, happiness and fear.

The children drew pictures of Wilson's family and put them in a book to form Wilson's family photo album.

Wilson with his tail

The teacher observed that she had found the children 'amazingly mature' in their discussion of 'being different' and 'being odd'. They recognised that, whoever you are and whatever you look like, you have the same basic needs such as food, clothing, shelter, families, love...

Further discussion could explore in what way physical features such as Wilson's tail, skin colour, physical characteristics and perhaps disabilities affect a person's feelings about him/herself and the world around him/her.

2. The Children's Families

The children were encouraged to bring photos of family groups, weddings etc. to school. They discussed *what makes a family* (In any class, there are likely to be members of a single parent families, children with step-sisters and brothers etc.) They also discussed similarities and differences both within and between families. For example:

- Do members of a family look like each other?

- In what ways might they differ?

- What do different families like doing? (One family may, for example, like going on picnics while another likes running a cafe.)

Resources

Long Blue Blazer by S. Willis.

What is a Family? (photopack) Development Education Centre Selly Oak College, Bristol Road, Birmingham.

The Three Bears

Background

An urban nursery school of 120 children located on two floors of a Victorian house. Practically all the children attend on a half time basis.

Aims: to develop the following Concepts, Skills and Attitudes:

- sharing
- co-operation
- sympathy
- learning to take turns
- learning to lead and to follow
- understanding differing needs of individuals
- understanding similarities and differences
- entering into the feelings of Goldilocks and the three bears

Process

1. The family of the three bears

The topic arose as an extension of work about families.

There were three aspects:

Me and my family

Me and other families (including bear families)

Me and Jesus' family

The topic was planned by working parties of teachers in weekly after-school sessions. Brainstorming helped build up possible ideas and from these a flow diagram was created as the starting point. The ten key curriculum areas (see flow diagram on page 00) were listed on separate cards and the staff linked the work in each area to the topic, using the ideas from the flow diagram. They were surprised at how many cross-references there were and how closely all ten areas fitted together.

At every stage parents and other people working in school were kept informed and were involved as much as possible. Parents offered their skills and loaned possessions.

2. Finding out about bears.

The children and staff found out all they could about bears, and brought their own teddy bears into school to add to those belonging to the school. They discussed the similarities and differences in both real and toy bears in terms of

colour

size

feel of the fur

habitat

food

3. The Three Bears

A teacher told the story of the three bears. Meanwhile two nursery nurses made three bear hats.

To the children's delight, the three teachers and a student then acted out the story. The children discussed the feelings of Goldilocks and the three bears.

4. Children's versions

A great deal of 'house' play followed. The teachers were interested to note that initially the children didn't use the three bears that had been put into the 'house', but preferred to act out the story themselves. They realised that there could only be three bears in the 'house' at one time and organised this themselves. 'Taking turns' is so much part of the school philosophy that there was no problem, but the power struggle between mummy and daddy bear was very evident, and the end of the story differed from group to group.

5. Eating activities

With some help from adults, the children made porridge. They ate it with honey, with sugar, with salt or with currants. (The children were just like bears in their taste for honey!) Though everyone tried not to get porridge on the walls and the floor, there were a few accidents and the caretaker nearly went up the wall!

Later, Ready Brek and a jug of milk were put in the house and the children made

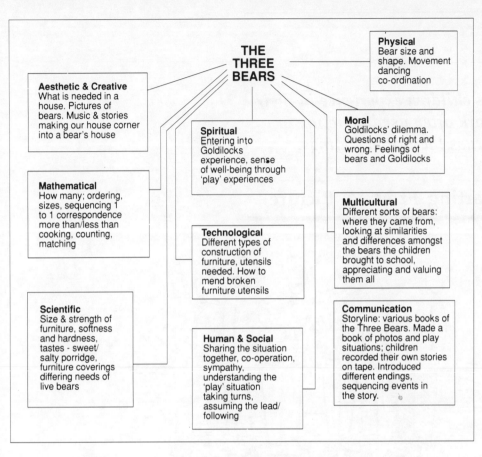

THE THREE BEARS

Physical
Bear size and shape. Movement dancing co-ordination

Aesthetic & Creative
What is needed in a house. Pictures of bears. Music & stories making our house corner into a bear's house

Moral
Goldilocks' dilemma. Questions of right and wrong. Feelings of bears and Goldilocks

Spiritual
Entering into Goldilocks experience, sense of well-being through 'play' experiences

Mathematical
How many; ordering, sizes, sequencing 1 to 1 correspondence more than/less than cooking, counting, matching

Multicultural
Different sorts of bears: where they came from, looking at similarities and differences amongst the bears the children brought to school, appreciating and valuing them all

Technological
Different types of construction of furniture, utensils needed. How to mend broken furniture utensils

Scientific
Size & strength of furniture, softness and hardness, tastes - sweet/ salty porridge, furniture coverings differing needs of live bears

Human & Social
Sharing the situation together, co-operation, sympathy, understanding the 'play' situation taking turns, assuming the lead/ following

Communication
Storyline: various books of the Three Bears. Made a book of photos and play situations; children recorded their own stories on tape. Introduced different endings, sequencing events in the story.

Flow Diagram

their own breakfast with as little help as possible from adults. They also learned to help with the clearing up.

6. Playing with the bears

As time went on, the children chose to play with the bears. Often they were seen with the bears on their laps, but by the end of three weeks, the topic had run its course and there were long periods when no-one played in the bear house.

Parental Reaction

Flow diagrams which communicate both the values and the curriculum of the school are always on display in the entrance hall of this school and parents are often seen studying them. A number of parents have commented and discussed them with the staff. They were very interested to see that the children 'didn't just play' and that the staff had worked out their plans and how they should be implemented carefully.

Opening up their work in this way made the staff very accessible but also gave them a marvellous opportunity to share their educational thinking.

It also resulted in offers of help:

> I've got some... at home, you could have.

> Would you like me to...?

The flow diagram of The Three Bears was displayed in the entrance hall.

Each curriculum area was written on a separate card.

An official visitor to the school challenged the identification of 'multicultural' as a separate area of the curriculum.

The headteacher's response was to stress that in a largely 'all-white' area like Cum-

bria, cultural diversity must be highlighted otherwise it will be ignored.

Comments

1. A well-loved story was used as a vehicle to extend the children's imaginations. The work with the teddy bears allowed the children a safe way into a consideration of difference. It may be possible to build on this experience by encouraging the children to talk openly about differences they see amongst themselves.

2. Although cultural diversity must be an important dimension of classroom work, perhaps the most important preparation for a multicultural perspective is the valuing of the experiences that children bring from home.

3. This school, for example, encourages close relationships between teachers, the home and the community.

SECTION V:
CONFLICTS AROUND US

Some ideas for getting into — and sometimes out of — the conflicts children experience in their daily lives are described in this section. Although the classroom work often used a picture or a story as a starting point, practically all the children wanted to discuss their own feelings.

18

Towards Conflict Resolution — Starting From A Picture

Background

A class of 10 and 11 year olds, 19 boys and 6 girls, in a small market town school, serving children from a variety of backgrounds.

Aims: to develop the following Concepts, Skills and Attitudes:

An understanding of:

• power and inequality

• similarities and differences, especially feelings

• conflict

A capability for:

• critical thinking and open-mindedness

• rational argument

• empathy

Process

1. **Introducing the picture.**
The children were shown the picture reproduced here.

i) The class were asked who they thought the group of boys were; whether they were friendly or hostile; what they were doing and thinking and what they were likely to do. Most of the class thought they were hostile because of the threatening shadows. All the children's answers were accepted as of value.

ii) The children were asked to visualise* themselves as the crouching boy and imagine how they would feel. After several minutes they were asked to open their eyes and were encouraged to share their 'experiences' with the rest of the class.

iii) A brainstorming session elicited words and phrases associated with:

• the group of boys

• their shadows

• the crouching boy

These were written on the blackboard and discussed.

* Visualisation: the children were asked to sit back on their chairs, feet flat on the floor and hands resting in their laps. Closing their eyes (not screwing them up) they were asked to take several slow deep breaths and then to visualise the scene.

2. Writing poems

The children were asked to write a poem that included any of the words listed on the blackboard.

It was agreed that they should write a short verse about each of the three aspects discussed.

Below are examples of their work.

3. Group discussion: Who helps?

Much of the work was done in small groups. These remained the same, allowing children an opportunity to get to know the feelings and ideas of four or five other children. This gave them the chance to develop their thinking over a period of time and lay foundations for long term action.

Each group discussed the following:

i) List some of the ways the crouching boy might protect himself.

ii) What advice would you give him?

iii) What kind of people might be involved in helping him?

4. Class discussion: The gang

The children raised the following points:

- They may not have been unfriendly, but because they were a group they were seen by the crouching boy as hostile/threatening.

- Another child questioned whether all the members of the gang had the same feelings.

- Was it right to assume that because the leader was hostile, all the rest of the gang were too?

- The children discussed what individual members might do to extricate themselves from the gang when or if they did not agree with the leader. Most of them decided they would make an excuse that they had to go home, so as to get out of any possible trouble.

Seven cruel, mean bullies,
A horrible glowering gang,
All crowded together there.
Mean, mocking and menacing.

Seven creepy shadows
Slithering across the ground,
Moving close to the little boy.
They're terrifying.

A little boy afraid, terrified
Of those big bullies coming to get him.
What will they do? Kick? Fight?
Why can't they forget him?

Elizabeth 10+

Seven unfriendly ruffians
Mocking the cowering boy.
Crowded together like a pack of wolves,
Leering at him.

The shadows slither softly,
Pointing towards him.
Snakes jump at the boy,
Bringing with them fear.

Sadly the boy crouches,
Rejected and unhappy,
Trying not to be frightened,
Although underneath he is.

Martin 10+......

.....They tap the boy's courage.

Their evil shadows creeping up
As vicious snakes do.
Like frightening alligators
They swarm around him.
Their savage faces striking terror
Into the small boy's heart.

He crouches down, lonely and frightened
As he sees the dangerous shadows
approaching.
He becomes apprehensive, worried,
His terrified heart senses one thing:
Doom!

James 10.

5. **Playing the part of the crouching boy.**
In a later session, groups prepared a role-play of the crouching boy's situation. They acted out what they considered to be the most satisfactory outcome, both immediate and long term.

The role-plays were acted out in front of the class.

Here are three examples:

i) A group of children playing ball refused to let one of the group go on playing because he was clumsy and kept dropping the ball. Later, one of the gang left to join the 'clumsy' boy because he felt he wasn't being treated fairly. Still later, he pleaded the boy's case and the gang allowed them both back.

ii) In a game of football, the goalie was so good that no-one could score a goal. The gang got jealous and frustrated, took the goalie's crisps, called him names and taunted him. He left them and went home. Next day the group realised they were being spiteful and called for him to come and play. He played football again and this time allowed a goal to be scored — ensuring acceptance by the group (!)

iii) In another game of football, there was considerable argument and when all the boys resorted to name-calling, the situation quickly deteriorated and they started fighting. The child who had started the name-calling because the others wouldn't let him play got hurt in the fight. He escaped and reported the matter to the head-teacher who sent for the gang and told them to make friends. They ignored this advice and lay in wait outside the injured boy's home. When he came out, they called him names and fought him: his arm was broken and he ended up in hospital. Members of the gang realised that they had gone too far and went to visit him.

After each role-play the rest of the class asked questions and made comments as to whether the problem, whatever it was deemed to be, had been resolved:

i) for the time being,

ii) in the long term,

iii) Whether other people who were brought into the role-play actually helped the crouching boy or a member of the gang.

When a child or the teacher identified weaknesses in the solutions offered, the teacher encouraged other children to suggest alternatives.

6. **Being rejected**
Each child wrote a personal account of what it feels like to be isolated, or rejected, or to feel lonely or threatened.

7. **Staff discussion: Are we really exploring inequality?**
The teacher realised that she needed to take the children's thinking further. As well as appreciating the situation of the crouching boy, she wanted the children to explore the feelings of groups who are rejected by society, for whatever reason. So plans were made for follow up:

8. **Picking up the threads**
i) The children recalled the probable feelings of the crouching boy and suggested he was:

lonely

dejected

frightened

petrified

left out

helpless

ii) They also recalled their role-plays and their ideas about the kinds of children who become the 'outsiders'.

9. **People who understand**
In their groups, the children were asked to consider two questions.

Two groups were given questions A1 and 2, and three groups were given B1 and 2. (The questions were phrased slightly differently because the teacher wanted to find out how to phrase questions most helpfully for the children.)

A1. **Who might be the adults/children who would understand your experiences when you feel down or an outsider?**

A2. **Why are they helpful?**

B1. **Who are the people who are most helpful when you feel down or an outsider?**

B2. **Why are they helpful?**

Without further discussion, the children completed this task in five or six minutes. Their sheets of answers were stuck on a large poster under the questions.

Here are the results:

Who are the people who are most helpful when you feel down or an outsider?
mum & DAD. friends, teacher, big brother, or sister. dog. Robert. Edward.

Why are they helpful?
to saught them out. they listen to them. They're bigger.

Who are the people who are most helpful when you feel down or an outsider?
Parents, Teachers, Friends, Other Family,

Why are they helpful?
Because they care about us and comfort us and love us.

Who might be the adults/children who would understand your experience when you feel down or an outsider? Mum & Dad. close friends, pets. teachers, Grans & Granpa's a child who's had that sort of experience

Why are they helpful? they sympathize, they sometimes understand how you feel,

Who are the people who are most helpful when you feel down or an outsider?
Parents, God. brothers and sisters. Teachers. Friends.

Why are they helpful?
Parents will tell you to stay away. Teachers will tell them off.

Who might be the adults/children who would understand your experience when you feel down or an outsider? Relatives &- parents. A child who has experienced the situation, Neighbours who have children your age,

Why are they helpful? Some people that have experienced the situation, They will know what to do.

The children read out their answers and had an opportunity to explain what they meant, or to expand their answers.

The idea emerged in discussion that the people who understand are often those who have had a similar experience.

10. Groups who feel threatened
The teacher said:

> There are groups of people in Cumbria, in Britain and in the world who feel threatened and weak like the crouching boy.

> Who are these groups?

Still in their groups, the children discussed this, wrote down as many answers as they could in five minutes and read them out before sticking their answer sheets onto a poster on which the statement and question had been written.

The five groups gave these answers.

Groups Of People Who Feel Threatened And Weak

> People who have lost there jobs. People that are abused. Black people ; White people, Skin heads, Gypsy, hippies.

> Blacks in S. Africa
> Chinese Students
> The people of Hong Kong
> The class ones on their first day of school
> Spastics

> Children at public schools, little children! Fat people and disabled people. People who suck thier thumbs, poor people, rich people, skinny people.

> Your Enemy
> Anybody And Everybody
> Sean and Ian
> Class Ones   (4-5 year olds)
> 1st Year Settlebeck (Secondary School)
> When you're on holiday and — you don't know anybody

> smaller people, people who aint very brainy. people who are new to school, who has moved house, a person by themselves, dwarfes, eskimoos, black people in a white land, ... old and cancer who know noone else has got it

The children then discussed why such groups should feel threatened.

11. Action for change.
The teacher reminded the class how individual children who had felt threatened had been helped. She asked the children how the groups who had felt theatened might help themselves or be helped.

Their answers included the following ideas:

> talking amongst themselves,

> getting together with other similar groups,

> taking the initiative and approaching the 'normal' people.

> keeping clear of people who threatened them.

12. Simulation: What do you do?
The teacher set the scene and asked each group to decide how they might react. They were encouraged to think of a variety of responses.

Scene:

> One evening some gypsies arrive on a site and park their trailer.
> Next morning a mother and her two children from the trailer go into the village shop. After a while they realise they are not being served but are being ignored.

Teacher to class: You are the mother. What do you do?

Discuss in groups.

Children's responses:

> Please may I...
> Excuse me...
> Get in the queue and ask to be served

> Get your food and put your money next to the till.

> There are equal rights in this country and we have a right to get served.

> Excuse me...(cough, cough) Can I have half a pound of bacon, please?

> Complain.
> Go to another shop.
> Ask politely to be served.
> Show the lady you have some money to pay.

Resources

Further work in the whole area of discrimination, prejudice, and people's rights may be found in:

World Studies 8-13 by David Hicks and Simon Fisher, Oliver and Boyd.

Minority Rights Group: *Prejudice*

Teaching about human rights Amnesty International Institute of Race Relations fact sheet on *Racism*.

Responses to bullying: work with a local writer

19

Background

This initiative involved 10 year olds in a County Junior School, a school serving a community which is amongst the most economically and socially disadvantage in the north of England.

Aims: to develop the following Concepts, Skills and Attitudes:

- understanding what bullying is and what causes it

- learning some positive ways of dealing with bullying

- appreciating justice and fairness

- valuing each other's contributions to discussion

- encouraging cooperation through group work

- communicating the group's findings to the rest of the class

Process

1.   A Local Author

John Murray, a local novelist, spent an afternoon in school working with the children on the theme of bullying. For the first ten minutes he talked about himself and his work as a writer. He showed the children some of his books; The children were really impressed by the one with his photo on the back.

2.   Memories of Bullying

John Murray told the children in some detail about an elderly couple he had known. The husband abused his wife both physically and verbally. Nothing she could do or say was ever right in her husband's eyes. When she cooked him a meal his comment would be, 'Do we have to have the same food every day?' If she prepared something new, he would find a way of complaining about that. The children listened intently and nodded — they all knew someone like that.

3.   Group Discussion on Bullying

After listening to John's memories, the class split into four groups, and each chose a leader and a secretary. Each group considered a different aspect of bullying:

i   **different ways you can bully people**

ii   **What could you do to stop someone bullying you?**

iii   **What sort of people usually bully others?**

iv   **What sort of people usually get bullied?**

After 10-15 minutes, each group reported to the whole class. General discussion followed. (The interest of the children was apparent by the way they were able to work in groups — a new experience for them — and by the level of classroom discussion.)

The following ideas emerged:

i.   **Different ways of bullying**
physical abuse and threats "If you don't, I will...
verbal abuse — name calling
emotional blackmail — refusing to be friends

ii.   **To stop bullying**
make friends with the bully,
give them sweets,
do what they say and they will leave you alone.

Some of the children realised that these were not very satisfactory answers. By opening up the discussion, the adults encouraged the following thinking:

Show the bully you don't mind and won't be scared,
stand up to him/her without fighting,
tell an adult if you can
avoid situations whenever you can
don't provoke bullying

iii.   **People who might bully**
people who aren't very clever,
people who haven't many friends,
people who've been hit themselves.
(Many of the children expressed the view that people who bully, often feel inadequate in some way themselves.)

iv. **People who might get bullied**
wimps
people who are different — to look
at, in their accent
people who are rather withdrawn,
cry easily, people who don't fit into
the macho image
people who are handicapped

From the level of discussion and involvement of all the children, their participation was clearly based on personal experience.

Future Work

i   The teacher felt that the children needed a more positive self- image to be able to challenge bullying behaviour.

ii Whenever there is a bullying incident, the teacher immediately makes time for the class to discuss the situation and find ways to respond to the needs of both victim and bully. They may be able to use some of the ideas put forward in the discussion with John Murray.

iii The children could use their work on bullying to analyse conflicts in their community and in the wider world.

Resources

Bullying in Schools ed by D. Tattum and D.A. Lane. Trentham Books

Can I stay in today, Miss? by C. Ross and A. Ryan. Trentham Books

Conflict Peace Pledge Union
Available from: Friends' House, Euston Rd, London NW1 5BJ.

Names and name-calling

20

Background:

An urban primary school with 195 on roll; a class of 28 10-11 year olds.

Aims: to develop the following Concepts, Skills and Attitudes:

- understanding

  similarities and differences

  the nature of conflict

- fostering

  a positive self-image

  open-mindedness

  an appreciation of other people's feelings

  respect for all individuals.

Process:

1. **Nicknames**
   i) Each child wrote their full name on the card. They underlined the name they like to be called. They wrote the abbreviated form they preferred.

   ii) With a partner they discussed how they felt about their full name and the name they liked others to use.

   iii) They wrote down any nicknames or derogatory names they had and discussed how they felt about them.

   iv) The children were very frank about the names they did not like to be called. They suggested that once we learnt what names others dislike, we should all stop using these names.

   v) The children considered some of the ways that adults describe children.

They included:

> *Hooligans, hoodlums, inconsiderate, disrespectful, cheeky, bad-mannered, noisy, nosey, outrageous, they get in the way.*

(The teacher wanted the children to talk about names. The children however, wanted to go beyond this and to discuss negative language in general.)

The children discussed what these terms might be based on. They talked about whether the names were true in part, or true about all children all of the time. They looked at how easy it was to stereotype any group and how misleading stereotyping can be.

2. **Children's responses to language used about them**

In small groups, the children considered these four questions:

   a) How do we feel when negative statements are made about us?

   b) How do we feel about positive statements?

   c) How important are names to how we feel about ourselves?

   d) How important is it for us to use positive language about other people?

3. **From negative to positive?**

The children chose several of the negative words from their list and transformed these into positive words which were discussed, for example, *cheeky* to: *asking, questioning.*

4. Name-calling: Immediate action

The teacher and the class decided that any future incident of name-calling should immediately be discussed by the whole class.

Name-calling is one of the most prevalent forms of abuse that children suffer. Any strategy that encourages children to reflect upon name-calling is desirable, especially if it results in children taking positive action to stop it. If children themselves are sensitive to name-calling amongst their peers, they are less likely to abuse others. They may also gain the confidence to challenge other children who call names.

Future Work

1. In small groups the children could consider whether it's possible to have a code of behaviour for the names used in school.

2. Name games. A variety of activities using children's names can be found in:

Resources:

'A feeling in my bones' Activity booklet, Theatre Centre

A manual on non-violence and children ed. by Stephanie Judson, New Society

Friendly Classroom for a Friendly planet by Priscilla Prutzman. Avery Publishing Group New Jersey, obtainable from: Friends Book Centre, Friends House Euston Rd., London NW1 2BJ.

SECTION VI:
WHAT'S IN A GANG?

This 'gang' work originated in a school in a large town in South Cumbria and involved school-based teachers and others working in multicultural, health and music education.

Glove gang and Nikers: creative conflict resolution

21

Background

This is a music workshop designed for 10-11 year olds. It was used by eight primary schools in South Cumbria.

A teacher questioned the relevance of multicultural education to his school, when his pupils found it difficult to get on with those from a school up the road. In discussion with others, he acknowledged that many of the important concepts, such as prejudice, conflict, inequality...fundamental to multicultural education, are those which children from any background relate to their own experiences. By exploring the children's own conflicts it may be possible to help them to gain some understanding of the nature of racism in our society.

Aims: to help children to deal with the kinds of conflict they experience every day and to develop the following Concepts, Skills and Attitudes:

- understanding concepts of conflict, violence and peace

- developing co-operation, respect and trust

- listening to each other

- understanding another's point of view, and questioning their own feelings

- evaluating a situation in the light of fresh information and trying to resolve issues of conflict peacefully, using music, drama and small group work.

- developing a sense of justice and fairness so that children are able to put forward reasoned arguments.

- analysing how a conflict is resolved and using the ideas in other situations.

- understanding the consequences of violence and the real possibilities of non-violent approaches.

- considering how the future may be shaped by the choices we make.

Process:

1. The children divided into two random groups. One group became the 'Glove gang', they wore goalies' soccer gloves. The other half became the 'Nikers gang', and wore Nike headbands and wristbands.

2. The groups separated and each learnt its gang song.

3. In their separate groups, the gangs spent time discussing conflict; about

- how each gang felt about its image

- how they might feel about the other gang

- what might bring them into conflict

- what might happen in this conflict.

4. The two groups came together with their identities as members of the Glove gang or Nikers gang firmly established and pooled their ideas about the gang conflict. The children chose which ideas to develop into a story. These formed the basis of their mini-opera. As they developed the story, they acted out the scenes.

5. Still in role, the children began to recognise how difficult it is to break the vicious circle of feuding.

Nikers Gang.

Ni-kers Ni-kers We're the Ni-kers Ni-kers Nikers Spe-cial

Ni-kers Nikers we're Ni-kers Bands of cloth up-on the head

Ni-kers Ni-kers We're the Ni-kers Cross the Nikers and you're dead

2. Nikers, Nikers, we're the Nikers
Nikers, Nikers, special club
Nikers, Nikers we're the Nikers
Bands of cloth upon our arms
Nikers, Nikers, we're the Nikers
See the Nikers special charms.

We are the Nikers

Untuned percussion

Xyl or Glock   D A D A D G D D

Chime Bars

Music by Kath Pearce   Greengate School.
Words by Colin Smith. Greengate School.

Glove Gang.

We are the glove gang glove gang glove gang We are the glove gang glove gang glove gang We a

brill gang brill gang brill gang we are a brill gang BRILL GANG

Fine to Coda

We always wear gloves to make a job neat You never know who you might meet in the street

[D.C. al Fine]

always wear gloves

Untuned Percussion

Xyl or Glock   D A D A D G D D

Chime Bars

Coda

We are a brill gang brill gang brill gang. We are a brill gang BRILL GANG

Music by Kath Pearce Greengate School.
Words by Colin Smith Greengate School.

Music by Kath Pearce Greengate School.
Words by Colin Smith. Greengate School.

To aid their thinking the teacher posed these questions:

What happens if:-

the Glove gang destroy the Niker's den?

the Nikers raid the Glove gang?

one gang takes a hostage?

and so on...

6. The gang members considered how they might break the stalemate. Their suggestions were woven into the story.

7. They symbolised the new understanding between the two gangs by sharing their headbands and gloves and singing a harmony song.

8. **Brainstorm**
The following day the children brainstormed the word **CONFLICT**.

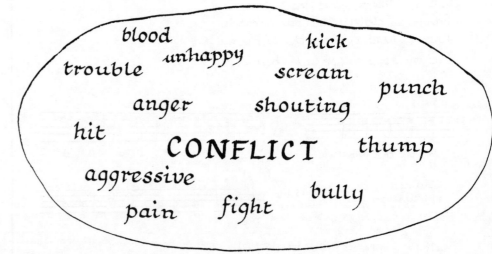

They watched the teacher tear the paper on which the words were written into two pieces, then described what she had done and what it meant.

Their replies included:-

split up... torn apart, divided, broke apart.

9. The children moved into groups of four each appointing a scribe. Using the brainstormed words and the children's reactions to the tearing as clues, each group worked on its own definition of the word *conflict*. After five minutes, each spokesperson shared their group's definition with the whole class, as they sat in a large circle. Something of worth was praised in each response, to encourage the children to feel positive towards themselves and others.

Their definitions:

> Conflict is when people fall apart or are separated because of things like fighting people disagreeing.. riots between black and white races. It happens between gangs and friends.

> Conflict is having disagreements with other people and fighting and suffering and sometimes death.

> Conflict is — fighting and bloodshed between people who disagree. Reasons for conflict are seperated familys or world leaders falling out.

> CONFLICT is an argument or fight when people get driven appart by disagreeing and takeing sides.

> Conflict is falling out. Some times you could fight. It breaks your heart. you can kill each other. get devorsed.

10. Picture activity

Each group was given a *conflict picture*, and a set of questions to discuss and resolve. Each chose a spokesperson and a scribe.

Their questions were:

a) Who is involved in the conflict in your picture?

b) How did the conflict start?

c) How do you think each person/side feels?

d) What might happen next?

e) Try to resolve the conflict so that each person/side feels happy.

Questions adapted from *Coping with Conflict* (see resources).

The groups discussed and wrote down answers to each question. To end the activity, a large circle was formed and a large version of each group's picture was shown to the whole class whilst each spokesperson reported their group's answers.

Further work

1. The following books contain many activities for promoting cooperation, conflict resolution, justice and fairness.

Human Rights by David Pike and Graham Selby. Mary Glasgow Publications.

Global Teacher Global Learner. by David Pike and Graham Selby. Hodder & Stoughton.

Earthrights by Sue Grieg, Graham Pike and David Selby W.W.F. Kogan Page.

One example used to good effect, is the bean bag activity in *Earthrights*:

> *Each child is given a bean bag to place on his/her head. They are not allowed to touch their own bean bag once it is in position. The children move round the room following the teacher's instructions;*

> *Walk...bend...turn*

> *The idea is that all the children must keep moving. If a bean bag falls to the floor, its owner has to freeze and cannot move until the bean bag is back in position. No other guidance is given. All must keep moving. How do they solve the problem? This activity is not possible unless people cooperate and perceive one another's needs.*

2. The ideas generated by the children could be used whenever conflict arises within the school context. The children listen to both sides of an argument and are involved in discussion about how they can resolve it creatively rather than with violence.

3. Children can explore conflict in the wider world, looking at newspapers and the television so that they can begin to feel an appropriate sense of responsibility and involvement in national and international situations. For instance, while learning about the issues in Northern Ireland, children may think an important step might be to build relationships with children in a Catholic school in their area.

Resources

Coping with Conflict Learning Development Aids.

22 Losing face

Background:

This workshop involved 9-11 year olds in a number of Cumbrian primary schools. Their locations were as various as Cumbria's landscapes, and included small rural schools and larger urban ones.

The workshops gave children a chance to explore group dynamics and to develop their assertiveness. Stages two to eight were run by three teachers, but one teacher did the rest. Stages two to eight took about two hours.

Aims: to develop the following Concepts, Skills and Attitudes:

- valuing themselves as individuals whilst showing respect and consideration for others

- perceiving what is needed to co-exist with others

- developing a deeper understanding of issues associated with choice and, in particular, how to say 'No'

- recognising one's own powers and limitations

- understanding the need for self-dicipline and self-control

Process:

1. Identity badges

The children used paper plates to make an identity badge for themselves. Some made patterns, Mark and Hannah drew pictures of their hobbies, and others wrote about themselves. Each badge, used later in the mini-opera, was unique.

2. Brainstorm 'Dangers in the environment'

In small groups, the children listed things in their environment that they saw as dangerous:

```
ROAD SAFETY,   POLLUTION,
FIRE, ELECTRICITY, WATER,
QUICKSAND, STRANGERS, ANI-
MALS, MUGGING, THE PARK,
GLUE SNIFFING, LITTER, VANDAL-
ISM.
```

The same issues appeared on the lists regardless of whether the children were in rural or urban locations.

3. Choosing the theme for the mini-opera.

The children decided to vote on which danger they considered to be the most worrying.

4. Insiders/outsiders.

The children's roles in the mini-opera were discussed before the play developed. They did this in three groups, each led by an adult. (see below)

'Insiders'	'Nobodies'	'Outsiders'
i) In the course of their play, the children symbolised the surrender of their identity to the gang by placing their badges inside a large box.	i) The children were given a choice of percussion instruments to accompany each gang chant.	i) They placed their badges on the outside of a large box to show that although they are gang members they are still individuals who may not always want to do the same thing as everyone else.
i) They make up a four-line chant to show their group identity and unity.	ii) They discussed the idea of choice.	ii) They make up a four-line chant to show their identity and unity.

The Chants

Chant 1

(eg We are the best gang we | all agree)

Chant 2

(eg Though we keep our motto we're | in-di-vi-du-als.)

Music for the chants by Kath Pearce © Greengate Junior School.

The Group Songs

Group 1 One group we stand united,   But all our parts are one
Group 2 Be   with us you've made your choice We all speak with one voice

Each cog makes up a slick machine. Our members look so mean and lean
No   one per son can break the rules. Or else you're out and look like fools

That to gether we can be a team.
If you want to think do that in schools.

Each group sings their verse individually to establish their beliefs.

The song can be sung as a canon as both groups sing simultaneously
Group 2 starting 2 bars later than Group 1 ie after Group 1 have sung "One group we stand united."

Percussion

One group we are best

Chime Bars

C E G
The whole song is based on the chord of C – so chords can be played on the beat.
Xyl or Glock can play notes in any order

Music by Kath Pearce © Greengate Junior School.

Words by Colin Smith © Greengate Junior School.

5. Coming together to develop their play

The Insiders and the Outsiders performed their chants, trying to persuade the 'nobodies' (who were accompanying them on percussion instruments) to join their respective gangs.

One by one the Nobodies slowly left their instruments, looked at and listened carefully to the two gangs, made their choices and placed their badges on either the outside or the inside of the boxes.

6. The group songs

The Outsiders performed their song to stress their identity. No sooner had they sung the first line than the Insiders began to belt out theirs (see page 68).

7. The plot

The two gangs, Insiders and Outsiders, were grouped separately in the room, each with a teacher to support their work. In their 'gang', the children discussed how the theme they had chosen from their list of environmental dangers might be woven into a play (fire... glue sniffing. .. litter...).

As the children developed the play in their roles, they began to bounce ideas off the other group. The teachers helped the children to develop their play by asking open-ended questions such as:

Teacher: When might fire be a danger?

Insiders: As a bonfire.

Teacher: What might the Insiders or Outsiders do?

Outsiders: We've built a bonfire for our firework display.

Insiders: We could wreck it.

Rap.

If possible have a rhythm section of a keyboard playing to keep the beat.

Chant rhythmically.

> It's easy to go with the affirmative
> Much harder to answer with a negative
> If everybody in the group says yes
> None of us has the guts, has the guts, I guess
> To an- swer no, oh yes, to an-swer no!

Percussion

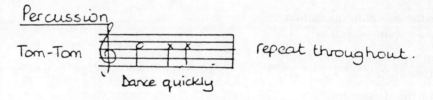

Tom-Tom — *Dance quickly* — repeat throughout.

Maracas - Shake on the last word of each line

Music by Kath Pearce © Greengate School.
Words by Colin Smith © Greengate School.

Teacher: In your Insider or Outsider groups, discuss what happens and whether all members of the group feel the same about it.

The children strongly identified with their roles as Insiders or Outsiders:

For example:

When two members of the Insider gang didn't want to destroy the other gang's bonfire, they were excluded. One gang member suggested that they 'scare em' a little to teach them a lesson by pushing them too near the bonfire.

The teacher asked the Outsiders to try to find ways of stopping this happening. The Outsiders immediately placed themselves round the bonfire so that they were between the fire and the Insiders.

As they worked through the gang scenarios, the children chose the event or solution that they liked best.

To get across the idea of reconciliation, the teachers asked questions such as:

How can we begin to find a way to resolve the situation?

How does this danger end?

Finally the two groups resolved an ending. It involved the children in learning a rap. (Rap has its roots in Afro-Caribbean culture. Rapping is a way of making talking into an art form with a definite beat). In one school, Amy wanted the Outsiders and their new friends from the Insiders group to sit round the bonfire singing the rap. Some children felt their allegiance to Insider group so strongly that they refused to join in with the larger group.

8. **Performance**
At the end of the day, the children performed their mini-opera to other children in the school.

9. **Strategies for coping with dangers.**
The next day, the children were given a number of situations, based on their list of dangers (see number 2 of processes). In small groups, they brainstormed their reactions.

Each spokesperson reported back to the whole class and the responses were discussed.

SITUATION:

FOR SEVERAL WEEKS YOUR GANG HAS TEASED A NEW MEMBER OF THE CLASS.

WHAT COULD YOU DO TO HELP?

Welcome him in.
~~Mak~~ Make frindes with him.
Show him around.
Stay with him ~~around~~ all the time
Make sure no ~~some one~~ picks on him.
Don't leave him out of all your games.

(Say what would you feel like if somebody was teaseing you.)

SITUATION:

AFTER SCHOOL ONE EVENING YOU ARE DARED TO PLAY "CHICKEN" OUTSIDE SCHOOL IN GREENGATE STREET.

WHAT CAN YOU DO?

go back in school and tell the teachers.
go to the shop and phone your mam
go to freind living on street

Tell the lolipop lady about it.   9 year olds.

10. Why don't we say 'No'?

In their small groups, the children considered what stops us saying 'No'.

Their responses included:-

Your mates make you do it.

You don't have the guts to say no.

A gang of lads might come and get you.

You might be scared because they might leave you on your own

You could be telling tales

We don't like upsetting our friends.

Our feelings.

Because you might not have anyone to play with.

You might want to have a go.

11. Practising saying 'NO'

The children worked in pairs as 'A' and 'B'. The A's were each given a slip of paper on which was written:

Give me a sweet.

They tried to get their partner, B, to say yes, but the B's had to keep refusing the request/demand.

The roles were reversed. This time, the statement read:

Hide this---

As a whole class, the children talked about ways they had tried to make their partners give in, and ways that they had used to say 'No'. Some of the children role-played their responses to highlight a particular point.

Alan showed how he said 'No' firmly, turned his back and slowly walked away when he was asked for a sweet.

12. Reflection

In a large circle, the teacher used a 'stilling' exercise to facilitate reflection on the play and activities. The children then wrote down one thing that they felt they had learnt.

Here are a few examples;

If you want to say no don't be scared just say it!

I say yes because I want to join in

I feel safe with my friends.

The following activities took place later:

13. Group dynamics

In small groups, the children looked at a large picture of the Crouching Child (see process 7 for a description of outsiders in children's play) and considered the following:

The gang

What do you think they are thinking?

How do you think they feel?

The boy (the children assumed the crouching person to be a boy)

What is the boy thinking?

How do you think he feels?

As a group, decide on a title for the picture.

The spokespersons reported the groups' answers to the whole class. Some discussion followed, the children challenging each other's comments or observations.

14. Role Play

Each small group began with physical postures that reflected the characters in the picture. They role-played solutions to the scene which they felt would:

- allow the crouching boy to protect himself and/or others to protect him:

- immediately

- in the future

The teacher and children discussed whether the solutions offered by their role-play gave short term and long term solutions.

All the children said that they had at some time felt like the crouching boy.

15. Keeping safe

In their small groups, the children wrote three rules that they felt would keep young people safe. The words *Don't* and *can't* were banned. They were to think in positive terms.

Here are some of their suggestions:

Keep away from big boys and girls.

I would advise you to stay near your home.

Be helpful.

Please no bullying.

We shall not hurt people's feelings.

Be safe with fireworks.

We will not play with people who gluesniff.

Please make friends with him or even leave him alone.

Keep away from that place where the gang hang out.

(9-10 year olds)

Future work:

1. The teacher could develop simulations where the children need to respond to racist remarks or behaviour such as:

You are in a football crowd and your mates start throwing banana skins at the black player.

How would you feel?

How would the black player feel?

How would the people throwing banana skins feel?

What could you do?
(Remember the skills in saying 'NO')

Resources:

Words & Music are the copyright of Colin Smith and Kath Pearce, Greengate School Greengate St., Barrow in Furness, Cumbria LA14 1BG.

SECTION VII:
INSIDERS... OUTSIDERS

Local communities and people are the framework for these projects, which consider responses to 'outsiders' and how people who appear 'different' may feel.

Micarbu

23

Background:

This primary school (50 on roll) is in an east Cumbrian village which appears at first sight to be a typical picturesque dormitory village; there is, in fact a large gypsum works at the back of the village and many of the parents work there. This project involved 8 and 9 year olds who worked on it over four afternoons.

Aims: to develop the following Concepts, Skills and Attitudes

an understanding of

- the concept of differences, in particular the various ways human beings can be classified
- the notion of stereotypes
- empathy, especially with people who may appear to be outsiders

Introduction

The headteacher of this school, herself a former advisory teacher for multicultural education, is concerned that the cultural mix of the local community should enrich the lives of the children rather than constitute an unspoken source of tension.

Process

1. Brainstorming 'differences'

Sitting round in a big circle, the children brainstormed all the ways people can be different. Their ideas, which were all written on a large poster, included:

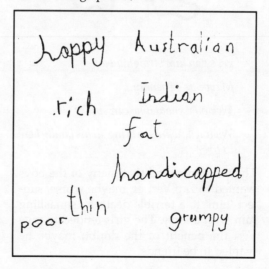

happy Australian
rich Indian
fat
handicapped
poor thin grumpy

2. Micarbu

In small groups, the children started to invent characters for a soap opera based on a village 'somewhere in Cumbria' called MICARBU. The teacher reminded them that human beings come in all varieties! As the

children began to understand that their imaginary villagers related to people they actually knew, they also worked out that MICARBU is an anagram of 'Cumbria'.

3. Frozen Moments

The groups presented their characters as *frozen moments* (the teacher 'freezes' the action when she feels that the characters are well into their roles). Other children then asked the 'frozen' characters questions:

Who are you?

What are you doing?

Why are you doing that?

What are you thinking?

How do you feel?

and so on...

4. Witches, Princesses and Princes

[At this point we decided to halt the process temporarily because we felt we hadn't given the children enough support in getting into their characters — mothers, eighty year olds, little boys were all behaving in very stereotypical ways!]

Before reading *Prince Amilec* all the children together brainstormed their ideas about witches, princesses and princes. They established that:

WITCHES
are horrible, spikey, black, creatures prone to cast evil spells which turn people into frogs

PRINCES
are handsome and brave, and that

PRINCESSES
'have no guts', they 'just lie around looking pretty'

When we read the story (see resources), the children's faces softened with amazement and delight as they realised that *this* witch was far from evil, while the princess had no intention of hanging around for a prince — she was off to travel the world!

5. Vert
The children dispersed into their small groups again and prepared to resume their MICARBU characters. This time each group was asked to dramatise a specific incident:

You are all out and about in MICARBU one fine sunny morning when suddenly you set eyes on VERT.

Each group opened a large newspaper envelope and found VERT.

For some minutes the groups worked through various responses to the presence of VERT in the village. It was already clear that this little green person inspired strong feelings! One by one the groups presented their 'frozen moments' and, by questioning the characters, the others found out what was going on in MICARBU.

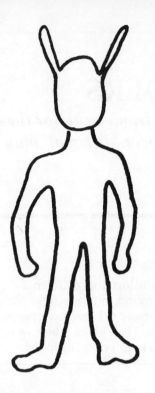

Let's zap him straightaway.

Maybe he's friendly.

We don't know if he can speak.

What if he wants to bring all his family here to live?

The teachers noted that many of the boys wanted to zap Vert or, maybe worse, subject 'him' to a terrible death by squashing him with a lorry. The girls tended to give Vert the benefit of the doubt: maybe he wanted to be friends.

6. What does Vert feel?
The children spent a few minutes discussing how Vert might be feeling now and drawing the appropriate expression on his face.

7. Other new people in the village
The teacher used the photopack *What is a Family?* to discuss the different sorts of people who might come and live in the village. It was fascinating to note that both girls *and* boys responded to photographs of young, perhaps unsupported mothers, by stating firmly that they would need a lot of help with children, shopping, etc. On being shown a photo of a fairly affluent young black (Afro-Carribean) woman, some children declared they would have to raise money for her... When the teacher suggested that she might be quite rich (there might be a BMW outside her house!) the children were still firmly resolved to treat her as a charity case.

8. Personal reflections
The project ended with a few minutes of quietness. The children closed their eyes and thought about any occasion when they might have felt different from the people around them.

Resources
Don't Bet on the Prince by Jack Zipes Gower Publ. Co. Ltd.

What is a Family? (Photopack) Development Education Centre, Selly Oak Colleges, Birmingham.

Further Work
An 'audit' of images in children's books might be a way to get into ideas of stereotyping. The children could, for example, explore to what extent the elderly, children, black people, women, families etc. they see portrayed are accurate representations. Do they match with the real people they know?

24

'Offcomers'
A simulation exercise

Background:

A class of 9-11 year olds, in a village primary school with 113 on roll.

Aims: to develop the following Concepts, Skills and Attitudes:

- understanding that people hold different values and beliefs

- looking at ways that groups are able to influence what happens within a community

- developing rational thinking and the ability to present an argument

- exploring the relationship between fact and opinion before making judgements, and being prepared to change our minds as we learn more

- providing an opportunity for pupils to find out more about issues related to living in a multicultural society

- developing open-mindedness

- exploring experientially the ideas of justice and fairness.

- valuing the democratic process

Process

1. Introduction.

The school is set in a village in South Cumbria. A shop in the village had been bought by an Asian family. Children on the playground were heard to say, *It's the last time we shop there*. Several other remarks were overheard that revealed prejudice and bigotry.

The Head decided that two things needed to be done:

- i) discover what the children really felt

- ii) tackle the situation by challenging prejudices by setting the children a specific task.

Task:

i) You are members of a village committee, I am the chairperson and I have a problem to discuss with you. You will have some time to think about the problem before you discuss it.

ii) As you know, ladies and gentlemen, over the last few months several (British Asian) families have moved into our village. I'm sure that, like me, you would like them to feel that they are very welcome. They can make, and have indeed made, a valuable contribution to our community.

iii) The main point of today's discussion is this: They would like to build their own place of worship on land adjoining the village and they have asked the committee for its approval.

The children were asked to role play their reactions. The pupils have a background of drama and so were accustomed to exploring their reactions through roleplay. They knew the ground rules and soon became 'hooked' into their parts. Being in role allowed the children to voice opinions they had heard. The chairperson challenged the children in a non-threatening way, asking them questions such as:-

Are you sure that's true?

How do you know this?

Creating a dramatic situation removed from their immediate experience enabled the children to express their sometimes very prejudiced attitudes.

Comments:

The level and the depth of the pupils' feelings and reactions was very telling, for example:

I know that it's alright really, but being honest I've got a funny feeling deep down about it.

One pupil argued, *'Of course it's alright'*, even when pushed and put under pressure by the chairperson (the teacher). Others saw the exercise as a chance to learn from each other. A couple of children worried about the village being unable to accomodate the needs of the 'offcomers':

Would the newcomers' style of worship affect the lives of the villagers?

The objections were really gut reactions rather than reasoned and logical.

It is important for this excersise to challenge some of the children's basic assumptions, for example. Is there a feeling that the Asian family is 'different', and that the white population of the village is 'all the same'?

The children could, for example, explore religious diversity within their community. (See *Diversity of Christian Places of Worship*. p79).

They would see how within Christianity there is a history of persecution of certain groups. For example Quakers in the seventeenth century were persecuted in that very area of South Cumbria and were sometimes assaulted and imprisoned.

25

People on the move

Background:

Ten and eleven year olds in a primary school with 183 on the roll, in a small coastal town.

Aims: to develop the following Concepts, Skills and Attitudes:

- understanding:

  other people's values and beliefs

  similarities and differences

  how power and inequality affect people

  the future in terms of hopes and fears

- developing open-mindedness and critical thinking

  empathy for those who were evacuated or left their homelands

- appreciating other cultures

- researching events in 'their' area before and during the war

Process

1. Introduction:

During the summer term, a class of 10 and 11 year olds looked at a number of linked topics, all of which had local relevance and which could be researched using local resources:

- the experiences of evacuees during the second world war;

- Jewish experiences: Judaism, the Holocaust and life in new countries;

- the experience of black people, in particular racial prejudice.

2. Mrs Koebner's Visit

The teacher invited a local Jewish woman to talk with the children about how she had left Nazi Germany and her subsequent life in Britain. Mrs Koebner asked beforehand what the children would want to know and she and the teacher discussed the problems and possibilities. They were both concerned that the children should be moved by learning about the Holocaust but that they would not be so frightened that they could not learn from the experience.

At the school, Mrs Koebner answered the children's questions. She described how difficult life had become for the Jews in the 1930s and how her parents had decided to stay in Germany but to send her to safety in England. Later her father died in a concentration camp while her mother escaped to Poland where she hid but finally died of hunger.

While her parents were alive, the only way she could correspond with them was through friends in Italy. When she first came to England, she was sent to a reform school, where her few personal possessions were stolen. She wasn't allowed to go to a secondary school and once war started, she was treated as an alien. Later she be-came a nurse and so wasn't confined like other aliens to the Isle of Man.

3. The Children's Reactions

The children tried to empathise with how it feels to be utterly abandoned, with no possessions or links with home and family. Because they had already done work on the position of evacuees during the war, they were able to make some connections.

The children were very moved at meeting someone who had suffered so much. Imagining themselves as evacuees or strangers, they wrote about their feelings.

I'M AN EVACUEE

Standing on a cold platform, tired with my spirits at their lowest ebb.
If I was a fly
I'd climb into a spider's web.
This morning it didn't seen so bad
As I waved goodbye to mum and dad.
Will anyone ever pick me
What's wrong with me?
Mummy used to say I was a nice little girl
With my fair curls
But she must have been wrong
Oh I hope I'm picked before long.
                    by KATHRYN BANKS J4

THE STRANGER

STANDING QUIETLY IN THE VERY DARK NIGHT

THE CHILDREN RUN AROUND HIM WITH DELIGHT

SHOUTING AND LAUGHING AT THE NEW BOY

THEY CALL; HIM NAMES JUST LIKE A TOY

HE COMES TO SCHOOL EARLY NEXT DAY

NOBODY WOULD LET HIM JOIN IN AND PLAY

AFTER A FEW DAYS HE MADE A FEW FRIENDS

THEN A NEW BOY CAME AND IT STARTED AGAIN

by JULIE SHARPE

4. Letters to Mrs Koebner

The children wrote to Mrs Koebner to thank her for coming to school and told her what had most moved and impressed them.

5. Anne Frank

When we read *The story of Anne Frank* (Pan), it had become much more real to the children as a result of Mrs. Koebner's visit.

> Cumbria
> 28th February
>
> Dear Mrs Koebner
>
> Thank you very much for coming to Bookwell. I enjoyed your talk alot my favourite part of it was when you told us about the day of rest and how mothers had to make the meals the day before. I was very sad when you told us how your parents were persecuted and how you had to live with total strangers.
>
> Yours sincerely
> Stephanie McKendry

SECTION VIII:
CHRISTIANITY AND DIVERSITY

Places of worship in Cumbria are mainly associated with one world faith — Christianity. By looking at the different ways people use churches, meeting houses etc. children can begin to develop a sense of the wide variety of religious practice in Britain and in the world.

The Diversity of Christian Places Of Worship

Background:

A class of ten and eleven year olds, 19 boys and 6 girls, in a small market town school which serves children from a variety of backgrounds.

Aims: to develop the following Concepts, Skills and Attitudes:

- *understanding something of the nature of religious belief and practices, and their importance and influence in the lives of believers.*

- *understanding some of the features of communities of faith*

- *expressing deep feelings and serious ideas appropriately and effectively*

- *appreciating that symbols and artefacts can express human feelings and ideas*

(These aims are drawn from Cumbria's Agreed Syllabus for Religious Education.) Also:

- encouraging pupils to question, search for meaning, reflect and understand

- providing support and assurance to any child who may belong to the faith community being studied

- recognising and appreciating the diversity that exists among Christians in five branches of the Christian church

- learning through experience by visiting places of worship and by meditating in them

- learning to work in pairs and small groups

- learning to communicate one's feelings and knowledge to the rest of the class

There is a variety of world religions practised in Britain but Cumbrian children don't usually have the opportunity to visit their places of worship. How then can these children learn about diversity of belief and practice?

We must start from the children's own experience and environment. We can learn that there is diversity among Christians. We can be interested in why and how Christians differ in their ways of worship. We can learn to understand, appreciate and

value diversity for the richness it creates in our society.

Having learnt that Christians worship in many different ways, children should, we hope, be more ready to accept the existence of other faiths, for example, Islam, and also of diversity within each faith. By showing that there are a wide range of interpretations within every faith, we can challenge stereotypes of Christians and believers of other faiths.

Process

(Each of the stages outlined below took about an hour).

1   **The starting point**
The teacher started from where the children were: what they knew and understood. To do this, she began by —

i)   brainstorming the word 'churches'. She discovered a wide- ranging knowledge amongst the children. The words they offered included:

> *Steeple, candle, choir, religion, celebrations, communion, Lent, Christmas, Sunday School, Easter, congregation, graveyard, pulpit, altar, God, Jesus, Bible, crucifix, cross, hymn books, holy water, font, statues...*

ii) She then discussed with the children many of the words that had been offered.

2 Visits to Places of worship

When they went into a church or chapel, the children would sit in pews apart from each other. They sat upright in an alert yet relaxed position with their feet flat on the floor and their hands relaxed in their laps. Initially they sat with eyes closed. (The children were used to such 'stilling exercises' in the classroom so had no difficulty behaving in this way in any of the places of worship.)

For a few moments they felt the atmosphere, noticing how their senses of smell and hearing were affected. Then they opened their eyes and looked around. Only then did they write down what particularly interested them.

As they sat there, they were asked to imagine what a worshipper might feel as s/he sat in that pew. The children walked round the place of worship and the teacher encouraged them to ask questions of each other, of her, or of a minister if present and to make observations. Each child also made a sketch of something that interested them.

The children visited the:

Anglican Church (also used by Roman Catholics)

Methodist Church

United Reform Church

Friends' Meeting House (Quakers)

3 Discussion following the visits

Discussions were mainly for the purpose of giving the children the opportunity to share and discuss their feelings in a sympathetic environment. The teacher read out some of the observations the children had written after their period of quiet in the places of worship.

For example:

> *This place is spooky with all the dead people buried here.*
>
> *People must feel sad when they come to pray about someone who is not here anymore.*
>
> *I think people would want to come here because it's quiet and it's easy to think.*
>
> *There's an absolute cleanliness and a humble sort of splendour.*
>
> *The banners on the wall help people to think.*

Back in the classroom the children examined posters and wrote down their questions. These were used as a basis for discussion. The children were encouraged to work in pairs. This stimulated discussion.

4 Using photographs and posters

The teacher displayed pictures showing different aspects of the interiors of Christian places of worship. Beside each was a sheet of paper on which the children, working in pairs, could write down their questions. These were later discussed by the whole class. Often the children were able to answer each other's questions.

5 Written work

Following the final visit, to a very old Friends' Meeting House, a small group of children made a list of the points of interest made by the whole class.

This group then used them in some free verse:

OUR VISIT TO BRIGFLATTS MEETING HOUSE

We walked through the small colourful garden to the entrance of the Quaker Meeting House.

There, over the porch, 1675...

We realised how old the building was.

The studded door was old but strong.

It stood open welcoming us.

We sat down quietly, our eyes closed,

sensing the atmosphere.

We looked around and could smell the old oak wood.

So many things interested us:

the balcony and its railings,

the rickety, uneven staircase,

the plain dull dark panelling,

the table with flowers and a Bible on it,

the long benches all facing the middle,

the visitors' book which some of us signed,

pictures painted of olden time,

an old marriage certificate,

the jams and biscuits for sale,

a tiny inscription on a small leaded window.

We shall remember the warden, Kimmett Edgar;

His interesting and amusing stories

which helped us understand the history of that place

Ninety minutes passed in a flash.

We had to leave to fit in a visit to Fox's Pulpit where he preached to so many Seekers.

How it rained. But we soon dried off on the journey back to school.

We are proud to think that this famous Meeting House is part of our Sedbergh.

6. **Further class discussion**

Tucked snugly in the book corner, the class discussed general questions about the visits, such as:

i) What did you find interesting about any visit? (The teacher thought everyone had found something of interest hence the positive nature of this question.)

ii) What were your feelings as you sat quietly in each place of worship?

iii) What similarities did you notice between the different places of worship?

iv) What were the main differences?

v) Do you think it's a good idea for Christians to have so many different kinds of places of worship? Why?

vi) Why do you think there are so many different kinds of places of worship?

viii) What do you think are the essentials for a Christian place of worship?

Class discussion about our visits to places of worship.

The children listed these:

> ## Essentials of a Christian Place of Worship
>
> 1. A Bible.
> 2. The right atmosphere.
> 3. People who are willing to worship.
> 4. People who care for the place of worship and are responsible for it.
> 5. Somewhere big enough.
> 6. Meetings to discuss important matters concerning the place of worship
> 7. A God.
> 8. Everyone belonging to that religion to be satisfied.
>
> (or, as another child put it:
> "They didn't argue.")

7. Chidren's thoughts about Religion

In small groups, the children discussed their thoughts about religion and then wrote them down.

> ## Our thoughts on Religion (Group 3)
>
> Peter thinks that there should be lots of different religions and churches because everybody's different.
>
> Elizabeth Maunder thinks that people should have the freedom to worship what they want.
>
> I think that there shouldn't be religion because it only causes wars and trouble. I think if there has to be a religion it should be like a big family. As well as this, it would help to stop nations fighting and to help all the world's countries to come together and be friends.
>
> Elizabeth Fell agrees with Peter and Libby, but she thinks the Quakers have a strange and much different way of doing things to other Christians.

8. Further Work

In 'mainly white' areas, this approach could form the basis of work on other world faiths.

Resources.

Exploring Religion series: *Buildings; Worship* by Olivia Bennett. Bell and Hyman (These books are useful for teaching about Christianity and other world faiths).

Christian Artefacts. Three colour illustrations with descriptive notes. Available from Christian Education Movement, Royal Buildings, Victoria Street, Derby DE1 1GW.

Exploring a theme series:
Places of worship
Signs and Symbols
Christian Education Movement

The Westhills project series:
Christianity Books 1-3, and Teacher's Manual. Mary Glasgow.

Christians Photopack 20 colour photographs in A3 format with background informa;tion. Available from Mary Glasgow Publications Ltd., Freepost, Bookhampton, Lan, Kineton, Warwick CV350BR

Believers all by David Simmonds, Blackie.

Believers: Worship in a Multi-Faith Community by C. Collonson & C. Miller. Ed. Arnold.

Pictorial Charts Educational Trust, 27 Kirchen Road, London, W13 DUD, has numerous sets of relevant charts and will send you a catalogue.

SECTION IX:
CELEBRATIONS AND OBSERVANCES

Celebrating a festival can put children at the wrong end of a telescope, studying the 'strange habits' of people 'out there'. Here, Chinese New Year was used as an opportunity to recognise the individuality and skills of one small boy. The all-encompassing theme of light led children in South Cumbrian schools towards an appreciation of some world faiths.

Celebrating Chinese New Year

27

Background
A class of four and five year olds in a village primary school.

Aims: to develop the following Concepts, Skills and Attitudes:
- helping a Chinese boy (four and a half years old) to feel accepted and to promote his self worth

- encouraging him to share his knowledge and experience of life in Hong Kong

- encouraging all the children to imagine themselves in another's shoes

- being aware of other people and their feelings

- developing forms of expression, verbal and non-verbal, appropriate to their experiences, feelings and thoughts

- learning about a Chinese festival

- encouraging an interested and questioning approach

- encouraging co-operation amongst the adults in the school community

- developing writing, painting, printing, and manipulative skills (including handling chopsticks!)

The teacher sought to involve parents as much as possible.

Process
1. Why Celebrate Chinese New Year?
Peter had recently arrived from Hong Kong and joined the reception class. The teacher encouraged him to show the other children some of the things he could do that they found difficult, for example, using chopsticks. From this developed the idea of learning about Chinese New Year, and this lasted most of the Spring Term. The aim was to locate it in as many areas of the curriculum as possible.

2. Using resources and involving parents
As most parents came into the classroom first thing each morning, there was plenty of opportunity to talk with them and they responded enthusiastically. The teacher asked parents to bring in Chinese artefacts.

The children watched and discussed a 'Playschool' programme on dragon dancing;

they made up their own dragon dance using Chinese music;

they learnt the song: *My ship sailed from China;*

they learnt to paint Chinese-style, after watching a demonstration by Peter's mother;

they made a class dragon using handprints on paper;

they practised using chopsticks;

they watched part of a holiday video made in Hong Kong lent by a parent, and

the school bought a Chinese doll for the 'house'.

3. Chinese New Year

The highlight of the half-term's work was celebrating Chinese New Year in the classroom. Cleaners and six parents helped with the preparations.

The teacher used drama blocks to make a low table in the middle of the classroom. On it she arranged cherry and apple blossom, tropical fruit and nuts, creating a strikingly beautiful centrepiece — a climax to the project. All the children's work had been arranged around the classroom, together with all the artefacts brought in by the parents.

The adults laid out 28 bowls, each with a pair of borrowed chopsticks. By this time most of the children could handle chopsticks with some degree of ease. The teacher put two hot plates in a playpen in the play area, safely away from the children. Two of the parents prepared a dish of stir-fry rice, chicken, beans and mushrooms. Another parent made gunpowder tea, lemon tea, and Jasmine and rose petal tea. Yet another recorded all the events on film.

Peter's mother brought in a car-load of clothes and artefacts, and children and adults all dressed up before sitting down to the meal, which they ate with their chopsticks, finishing with fresh lychees and clementines.

The following week, the children took an assembly in which they shared with the rest of the school their knowledge and appreciation of Chinese New Year.

Comments

From the children's remarks it was clear that they were forming positive images of Chinese people.

The children gained satisfaction from achieving a certain competence, able to do things they had seen and heard about.

Eating Chinese food stimulated an appreciation of unfamiliar food and drink and lessened the possibility of such experiences being viewed as exotic and showy, emphasizing rather a common basic need.

Further work

Use the 'Giant Chopsticks' story to reinforce the notion of co-operation. This is told in:
Co-operating for a Change City of Newcastle upon Tyne 1SBN 092653547

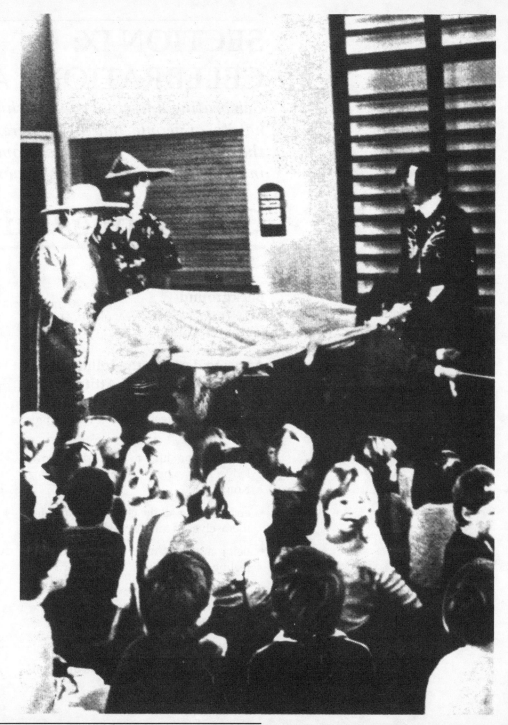

28

Divali — A Festival Of Light

Background

The school serves a small rural community in West Cumbria. Its 31 pupils are drawn from nearby villages and isolated farms. The Infant Class in which the project took place has 15 children aged from 4 to 7 years.

Aims: — to develop the following Concepts, Skills and Attitudes:

- knowing that festivals are celebrated by people throughout the world

- relating their own preparation for Christmas to winter light celebrations in other cultures

- understanding the central importance of the family in any celebration

- learning that the majority of people in the world do not celebrate Christmas and that *their* customs and traditions be respected and not treated as 'odd'

Process

1. Discussion about light

The teacher led a discussion based on the questions:

Why do we need light?

What gives us light?

What would happen if there were no light?

Why do people all over the world have celebrations about light? (The obvious starting point was birthday candles.) See 'Resources' list for materials used.

2. Rama and Sita

The children listened entranced whilst the teacher told this traditional tale of the triumph of good over evil. She stressed that this story was from India and that in Britain we can luckily hear stories from many parts of the world.

The children looked at and talked about Rangoli patterns, which are used in the Hindu Festival of Light, Divali.

Traditional Rangoli Patterns.

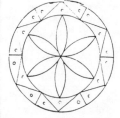

With the help of a local potter, the children made clay pinch-pot *divas*, the traditional Indian candle holder. Then they decorated them with simplified versions of traditional designs.

Divali (or Diwali) is a Hindu festival during which homes are lit with numerous tiny clay lamps called *divas*. Divali commemorates Rama's defeat of Ravana, the demon. The divas symbolise the victory of light and goodness over darkness and evil. At Divali, Hindus draw *Rangoli* patterns which are thought to bring good luck. They are usually drawn on the ground outside the door, with rice flour and spices or coloured chalks.

3. Looking at the Stars

An amateur astronomer showed the children a number of constellations, and the children learned about stars and star grouping:- The Plough, Orion the Hunter, the Seven Sisters... They learned that the same constellations look different depending on where in the world one is standing. The children can discover this for themselves by the following practical exercise:

Making 'The Plough'

The children cut out the seven stars of the Plough, colour each differently and hang them from the ceiling in the shape of the Plough. They then stand in different parts of the room and draw what they see. However accurate these representations may be, each will be different. Similarly, we all live in the same world but we see different aspects of it, and have different ways of viewing it.

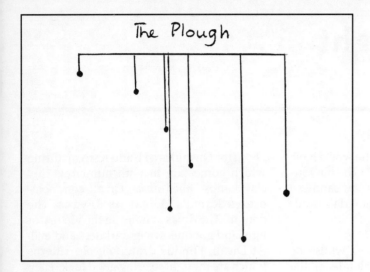

The Plough

Resources

Divali in the *Celebration* Series. Ginn 360
Reading level 10. 1985

Divali in the *Festivals series* by Olivia Bennett. Macmillan, 1986

Festivals in World Religions ed. Alan Brown. Longman, 1986

Festivals in the *Exploring Religion series* by Olivia Bennett. Bell and Hyman, 1984

Exploring a Theme series: *Festivals of Light.* Christian Education Movement, Royal Buildings, Victoria St. Derby DE1 1GW

A CUMBRIAN TEACHER'S PLAN FOR INFANT SCIENCE

Attainment Targets for a topic on LIGHT

To develop a strong multicultural dimension, the teacher can use the topic content to foster certain attitudes. For example, in the practical work on constellations described, the children learned that the same phenomenon can be seen differently and that each person's view is valid.

Attainment target	Level 1	Level 2	Level 3
1. Exploration of science	Handling clay. Making divas. Group discussion during process	Speculation. What would happen to flame without oxygen?	
2. Variety of life			
3. Process of life			
4. Genetics of evolution	Appreciating similarities and differences in their own appearances: hair, skin, eyes, etc.		
5. Human influences			
6. Types of uses of materials	Handling clay modelling	What happens when clay hardens? Observation of melting wax for candles	
9. Earth and atmosphere	Observation of stars cloudy/frosty nights Difference in climate		
10. Forces			
11. Electricity and magnetism	Lighting in houses Street lighting	Need to treat electricity with respect. Overhead powerlines	Constructed working model of lighthouse circuits
12. I.T.			
13. Energy			
14. Sound and Music			
15. Light	Natural light — stars, moon, sun, differences between candles/electricity	Shadow puppets (Divali) Observation drawing of candles	Constructing *simple* Kaleidescopes
16. Earth and Space	Discussions about sun as source of light	Simple discussion of planets. Display of constellations	
A response to DES *Science in the National Curriculum*			

29

Hanukah — A Winter Festival Of Light

Background

The topic was planned for the five and six year olds in a two teacher village Church of England primary school.

Aims: to develop the following Concepts, Skills and Attitudes:

- understanding something of the festival of Hanukah

- understanding that all people may celebrate festivals and light is often a feature

- understanding and accepting that different people see and do things differently

- co-operating in the making of the menorah (Hanukah)

- problem solving regarding the best way to make a menorah

- listening to each others' ideas

Process:

1. Identifying the topic.

The teacher had thought of LIGHT as the vehicle for developing some of the above Concepts, Skills and Attitudes.

The topics associated with Light could be:

Hanukah (Jewish)

Divali (Hindu)

Jesus, Light of the World (Christian)

Christingle (Christian)

Candles — used by all the above.

Below, we show how the teacher develops the Hanukah theme:

2. Introducing Hanukah

Hearing about the origins of Hanukah fascinated the children. They learnt why Jewish people celebrate it today. After some discussion and questions, the children all contributed to a joint piece of writing, using the computer.

3. Making a Menorah

The children were set the task of constructing a menorah, working in small groups.

When dividing them into groups of three or four, the teacher took care that the two most articulate children were in the same group, so they could challenge each other rather than dominate two separate groups.

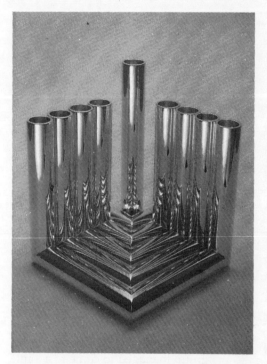

Hanukkah lamp 1980. Yaakov Greenvurcel.

Children were given time to think up their own ideas before discussing these with the rest of their group. After much questioning and argument, each group decided how they would make their Menorah.

The teacher stood back and observed these discussions, noting exchanges such as:

'We'll do it my way. Yours won't work.'

'Yes, it will.'

'How?' (Explanation given.) 'No, it won't work because the candles will set fire to the box.'

'Well, what's your way?' (Explanation followed.)

'No, that won't work, because the candles will drop through the top of the box.'

'No, they won't. I'll make the holes too small at first so we can get it right.'

4. Using the Menorah

After completing the group menorahs, the children spent a lesson lighting them and learning the customs associated with their lighting.

They learnt how to use the shamash (the servant candle) to light the other candles in the prescribed order.

Every child was given an opportunity to light one or more candles — and to blow them out.

Teacher's Observations

i) Each group took much longer discussing how to make the Menorah than in the making of it.

ii) It was interesting to see how each group managed to come to a joint decision through discussion. No-one actually lost their temper!

iii) Each group made a remarkably presentable menorah which could be lit in safety, and no group found it necessary to call on the teacher for help.

iv) Surprisingly, one pupil had no idea how to blow, never mind blow out a candle. There are still things to learn about children!

v) The children became aware that Jewish people celebrate Hanukah each winter. But the custom was new to them. They accepted that different groups of people do different things, and that 'that's O.K.'.

Resources

Exploring Religion series: *Festivals* by Olivia Bennett. Bell & Hyman.

The Living Festival series: *Chanukah* by Lynne Schofield. R.M.E.P.

Celebrations series: *Hanukah* 360 Reading Scheme. Level 10. Ginn.

All about Jewish Holidays and Customs by Morris Epstein. Ktav Publishing House.

The Jewish Kids Catalogue by Chaya M. Burstein. The Jewish Publication Society of America.

Hannukah by M. Schlein, Behrman House, (The last three books are available from:

The Jewish Education Bureau, 8 Westcombe Avenue, Leeds LS 10.

(The word 'Hanukah' is transliterated from the Hebrew, so there will be more than one 'correct' spelling in the roman alphabet.)

SECTION X:
OTHER PEOPLE... OTHER COUNTRIES

These units attempt to explore some of the assumptions children may hold and to develop empathy with the feelings of victims of racism and other injustices.

Hiding a People's History

30

Background

The work described here involved a class of 9-10 year olds in an urban junior school around the time of the bicentennial celebrations in Australia and helped the children to see what was 'hidden from history'.

Aims: to develop the following Concepts, Skills and Attitudes

* understanding:

  the values and beliefs of another people

  the conflict between power and equality

  similarities and differences between groups

  justice and fairness

* empathising with:

  other people's feelings

  an aboriginal point of view

* appreciating other cultures

* using media and television presentations to extract relevant information

* developing open-mindedness and critical thinking

Process:

1. **Ways in which we plan to develop the topic across the curriculum**
   (See diagram overleaf)

2. **Role reversal.**
   The children were given a choice of situations to discuss in small groups. Here are two of them:

   > You are English: How would you feel if the Aborigines made you take your clothes off?

   > How would you feel if strangers arrived and began to dig up your garden/park/playground?

   For many years the aborigines have had to respond to the actions of alien cultures. The children had an opportunity to empathise with the aborigines through role-playing similar experiences.

Aborigines

I am a settler on my way to Australia.

I am going to see the Aborigines,

I will teach them different ways

it will take me a lot of days

they don't have to do what I say but

if they like it they will have to repay

they can lead their own lives

in pain and in strife.

I don't think it is very nice

for they have a good life

but the other settlers don't agree

that they should be set free

and lead their own lives once again

they will always be in pain again and again

until they are set free

10 year old

WAYS IN WHICH WE PLAN TO DEVELOP THE TOPIC ACROSS THE CURRICULUM

TERM _____ Class _____ Signed _____

Humanities

GEOGRAPHY

Political, physical, climate
Artifacts
Education, Flying Doctor, radio
Communication
Coral reef, deserts, swamps,
Evergreens, decidious, forests. Why?
The Coastline
Flora/fauna/wildlife
Marsupials
Communications
Roads, rail, boat
Time difference
Lifestyle, food, crops etc.

HISTORY

Aboriginies and their life style
Now and past
The Early Settlers
Convicts
Modern cities
A modern country v England
Ships
Tools

R.E.

The Aborigines - their spiritual past/present
Dreamtime
Walkabout

THE CASE
Aborigines v Early Settlers
Aborigines v Present day pressures
Empathy

ART & CRAFT

Colour tints/shades
Australian scenes
Landscapes
Craft work:
Rock/stone painting
Bare painting
Driftwood sculpture

TOPIC - AUSTRALIA

P.E.
Ball skills
Ball and surface angle
Ball and game related skills
Ball awareness

MUSIC
Traditional/Modern
Aboriginal folk
Story type
composed by groups
based on traditional
aboriginal music.

LANGUAGE

Speech
Reported Events
(TV)
Conversation
Stories - RE.
Aboriginal feelings,
settlers, conflicts.
Cross-reference to
other curriculum areas

MATHEMATICS

Scale
Area
Comparison/estimation
Length
Time - 24 hour clock
and Time Zone
SMP
C & L

SCIENCE

Water and Heat
Condensation
Evaporation
Erosion
Weathering
Sediments

extensive
use of media
(TV/video)
to illustrate
appropriate areas
of work especially. RE/Music
descriptive work. Geography.
Schools Radio Coverage

3. Images

The children looked at lots of images of aboriginal life — at body paintings, families on walkabout, people in chains. They also learned about the dreamtime and its importance in the people's lives. In response to these stimuli, the children wrote poems and prose, which they illustrated. Their work —'The Black Argument' — was mounted together with the original images, on black, white and red card and the result was a powerful statement.

4. Feelings

The pupils explored what their feelings might be in a range of situations, for example:

> If you were out playing and some strangers came and took you away in chains, without letting you even see your parents, how do you think you would feel?

> A small group did a visualisation of what it might feel like to be an Aborigine, and then wrote about their feelings.

Examples of work by 10 year olds.

I was sat under a tree when I saw something run very fast past me then it stopped and made a funny sound like a bark. I said to myself 'What is that it does not live here?' So I started to run, there were some more coming and they caught me and made me wear silly things on my feet, a silly hat and silly clothes then they made me go to school. I tried to run away but they put a big fence around our tribal area.

Karen Armes

If I was an Aborigine and the white settlers came I would feel scared, unhappy and worried if they came over and Demanded me to put Clothes on I wouldn't, I would tell them to be friends with me I want to be friends so I asked them very kindly not to dig up the rock because of the spirits but they said they had to for treasure So they surruoned me. but I told them to look behind and I crawled under their legs ran to the water and drowned.

If I was an Aborigines I would be scared and angry when the white people came and shot a kangaroo with a long stick It they wanted to take the home of the spirits and if they tried to make me wear long dresses and jumpers I would be very unhappy. I tried to run away but they had put strange barriers around my home. The white people were strange they had strange things on their feet. They tried to make me put things on my feet and body I was very unhappy but I put them on in the end. They made work but I would not do it, in the end I did it and I was very unhappy. They gave me strange food. I lived a very unhappy life

Joanne.

200 years ago convicts were sent Australia. When they got to Australia they saw dark people. They said these people shouldn't dress like this. They should dress in clothes like us. So they forced the Aborigines to wear clothes and do the things that we do. The English people chained the Aborigines up. If I was in that situation. I would try and make them understand that we eats and dress different and it is our way of life.

- human dignity
- oneness with the earth;
- respect for all life:

The children were obviously impressed by aboriginal land values: that the world belongs to everybody; that no one has the right to own land because it belongs to all, but that all should respect it. They began to

and the same race, our race. (Chief Seattle 1849 letter to great white chief).

Everyone likes to give as well as receive. No-one wishes to receive all the time. We have taken so much from your culture, I wish you had taken something from our culture...For there were some good and beautiful things in it... (Chief Dan George.)

5. Discussion

i) The children had discovered that aboriginal people sometimes decorate their bodies by burning patterns with hot ashes, and as they discussed this with their teacher, he noticed that several of them also had self-inflicted cuts for precisely the opposite reasons: mutilation, not decoration. The teacher became determined that future work should emphasise and enhance the children's self-esteem.

ii) While looking at the pictures of traditional aboriginal life, the children demonstrated their recognition and appreciation of the aborigines'

- sense of pride and identity and its expression by body decoration,

compare this with our materialistic culture and its lack of respect for the oneness of the earth and all living things.

Future Work:

1. The idea that we can learn from other cultures and so about our own, may provide direction for future work.

2. The theme 'respect for all life' can be found in other cultures, for example the Native American:

We are part of the earth and the earth is part of us. The fragrant flowers are our sisters, the reindeer, the horse, the great eagle, our brothers. The foamy crest of waves in the river, the sap of the meadow flowers, the pony sweat and the man's sweat are all one

3. It may be useful to concentrate on Native Americans to develop work that challenges stereotypes.
   A plan might look like this;

   i) Brainstorm the term 'Red Indian'.

   ii) Children's thinking may be guided by asking them:

   - Where do these images come from?
   - Are they true?

   iv) Providing images created by Native Americans or children.

   v) Develop empathy by working in small groups on the exercise, 'Native Americans Today' on page 123-124 of *World Studies 8-13*

Resources:

World Studies 8-13; A Teacher's Handbook by Simon Fisher and David Hicks. Oliver & Boyd.

Poster of quotations. Development Education Centre, Selly Oak, Birmingham.

31 Images Of Kenya: Challenging Stereotypes

Background:

A class of 10 year olds in a county primary school. The children come from an extremely wide range of socio-economic backgrounds and bring to school widely differing experiences.

Aims: to develop the following Concepts, Skills and Attitudes:

- openmindedness, curiosity, critical thinking

- self-worth and acknowledging the worth of others

- appreciation of cultural diversity

- empathy with people in Kenya

- understanding similarities and differences between people, particularly with regard to clothes, climate, buildings, schools.

- notions of interdependence

- understanding of social change, for example the effects of road building schemes, farm cooperatives, rural craft ventures.

Process

1. Introduction

The focus for the term was *It's our Earth and It's Changing*, looking at environmental issues in Kenya and in the UK. As part of this work, the teacher brought in some artefacts that her husband had brought back from Kenya, together with a request from a school there for pen-friends in England.

The children painted pictures of what they thought Kenya was like and they had a brainstorming session on AFRICA. Mud huts, grass skirts, lions and spears abounded.

2. A Visitor who had lived in Kenya for seven years.

i) To set the scene for the first lesson, the teacher asked the children to write down in five minutes (working in pairs) what they felt were the essential needs of human beings. Their lists, which they read out, included:

> *food, drink, sun, shelter, clothing, friendship, family.*

By listening in to these discussions, the two adults got some insight into how the children arrived at their conclusions.

Recent work with children in Cumbria suggested that many of them have stereotypical images of Africa and Africans, believing them to be helpless, starving and waiting for Western aid to 'save' them. It is important that children are made aware that countries in the 'third world' have the same variety of life styles as other countries.

ii) The visitor asked if all human being shared those needs wherever they lived. She then asked why needs are satisfied in so many different ways.

Why are some houses made of stone and others of brick or mud and wattle?

Why do some people wear thick clothes, boots and gloves, while others wear shorts and tee shirts?

Gradually some of the children began to articulate that climate, habitat, raw materials, and equality of opportunity all play a part in determining how people live.

iii) The visitor used her slides of Kenya to show something of the diversity of lifestyles, of landscape, buildings and clothing, some of the many crops — both subsistence and cash, markets, buildings, including schools made of mud and wattle with corrugated iron roofing, built by the parents as part of a 'Harambee' (self help) scheme. There were also slides of schools very similar in style and equipment to modern British schools. The children saw rural houses built of local materials, and multistorey buildings in Nairobi. They saw shambas (small cultivated plots) where people were using hand tools, and they saw large industrial concerns.

During the slide show, the children asked such questions as:

Do Kenyans mind the heat?

Do the Tribes fight each other?

Why are they terracing the side of the hill?

Why are some shambas very green and others brown?

Do all Kenyans have a shamba?

They began to see how misleading stereotyping can be.

Some of the slides showed the creativity of different communities: the beautifully polished carvings of the Kamba people; the brightly patterned sisal baskets and mats of the Kikuyu; the highly decorative bead and leather work of the Masai, and they were full of admiration for the way school children modelled human and animal figures out of banana fibre, sticks and thorns.

Future Work

1. After examining artefacts from Kenya, the children could design and make objects of their own, using wax resist dying, clay, raffia and paint.

2. Having thought about the richness and complexity of life in Kenya, children could role-play situations, for example, a village discussing its water problems, a community accepting a tractor from an aid agency.

Resources

Images of Africa Development Education Project c/o Manchester Polytechnic, 801 Wilmslow Road, Manchester M20 8RG — a slide set and book of classroom activities which challenge stereotypes — a good antidote to the racist images and assumptions evident in some charity publications.

Materials from the Commonwealth Institute Kensington High Street London W8 6NQ.

(The Commonwealth Institute has an Educational Resources Centre from which items can be borrowed free, with a small charge for postage. The subject areas include:

agriculture
art/crafts
cookery/food

festivals
geography
history

life styles
music
religion

rural life
tourism
urban life

Simulation games might be used to look at unequal trade relations between rich and poor countries. These are available from Oxfam, War on Want, Christian Aid and Development Education Centres.

From Kendal to the Ganges

32

Background

This topic involved two classes of nine year olds. The children were from a large town school and many of them had participated in 'twinning' with children from either an inner city school or another Cumbrian school. The topic lasted half a term.

Aims: to develop the following Concepts, Skills and Attitudes:

- understanding: similarities and differences within a country as well as between countries:

    why and how changes take place

    what is meant by culture, religion, stereotypes, and interdependence

    seeing their own lives in a world context

- learning to use atlases and maps

- appreciating one's own culture and that of other people

- developing empathy and curiosity

Process

1. Choosing artefacts

In groups of six the children were asked to select any five objects that could represent their classroom, and put them into a box.

Each box became an artefacts box, to be used by Indian children to learn about an English classroom and what happens in it.

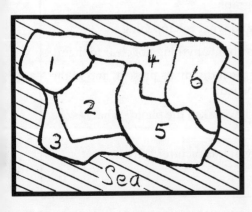

2. Examining the relevance

The groups shared their findings and produced a graph indicating the five most popular objects. They were:

    paper

    books

    pencils

    paint

    paint brushes

The children soon realised how difficult it was to represent a place or group of people by using one limited selection of objects. They agreed that the five most popular items they had chosen were so common world-wide that they would hardly be distinctive to an English classroom In discussion, the children said they needed special items to be distinctive, but realised that such items by themselves were equally misleading.

3. Widening the brief

The children repeated the exercise but individually this time, seeking to represent their own bedroom or home by five objects. Then they tried to compile a list of five objects or pictures with which to represent the UK. Again they were convinced that, however clear the images, they would provide a very inadequate picture of the UK.

4. Indian objects

The teacher showed them an Indian box that she had. It contained:

    rice

    a sari

    incense

    garlands

    a picture of a sandy beach

The objects were handed round and closely examined — looking, touching and smelling. In their discussion, the children were agreed that this box, too, had severe limitations.

5. Map work

i) They began by identifying where Kendal was on a map of the UK; where the UK was on a map of Europe, and then on a map of the world. They looked at some of the features, for instance: the relative size of countries; how some countries bordered on several other countries...

ii) *Making our own country*. On a large piece of paper, the teacher had drawn an imaginary continent, dividing it into six countries, one of which was land-locked. She cut out the 'countries', and gave one to each group. They were each asked to describe their 'country', using the following questions as starting points:

- What do the people do?
- How do they survive?
- Where do they live?

Each group drew pictures and symbols on their maps which illustrated and summarised their discussion. The elements common to all groups were:

- people
- government
- law
- shelter
- education
- animals

6. Isolation

In their groups, the children discussed what problems their country would face if it were isolated from all other countries.

7. Interdependence

The children reassembled their 'countries' into the 'continent' and discovered that they all had borders with other countries. In their groups they discussed the advantages and disadvantages of this and what responsibilities were created by such close proximity.

8. Individual work.

Each child chose one of the seven elements that all the groups had considered essential in the making up of a country. They had to relate it to India. Using their research skills, they found out all they could from the vast a..ount of resources which had been collected and borrowed. The County Project Library and local Teachers' Centre were very helpful.

The children spent two lessons in research and a third writing up their findings.

The children who had chosen *food* cooked traditional Indian recipes with the help of a parent, and then shared their food with the rest of the class.

9. From Kendal to the Ganges

Using maps and slides, the children planned a journey from Kendal to the Ganges. They role played:

a) booking their tickets

b) travelling by land, sea and air

c) their feelings at the end of the journey.

10. In India

Each child was given a picture of an Indian scene and invited to imagine themselves in the picture, and notice as much as possible about the scene. Then they were asked:

What can you see?

What questions do *you* want to ask?

On the right are three examples of their responses.

11. Sharing their 'experiences'

All the children talked about their pictures. Their questions and comments informed the class discussion.

12. Science

i) The children looked at, smelt, tasted and described some Indian spices. They ground the whole spices and compared them before and after grinding.

ii) Then, using the spices, they made:

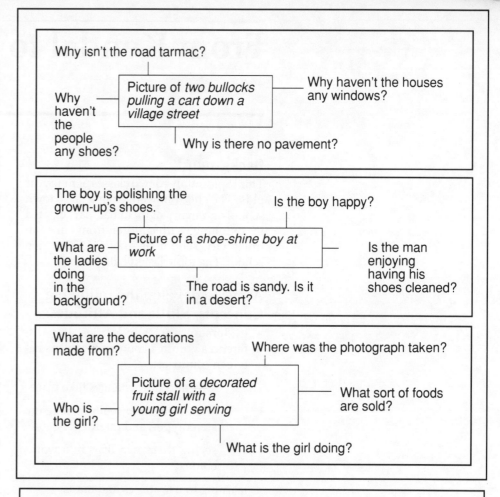

SOME SUGGESTIONS FOR HELPING CHILDREN TO 'READ' A PHOTOGRAPH

1. Give a general description of the photograph.

2. Say who and what objects are present, and what is happening.

3. Encourage the children to ask questions about anything not clear to them.

4. Ask children to imagine the feelings of the individuals present, and of the possible events leading up to the scene depicted.

5. Investigate why the photographer may have taken the photo. What is s/he trying to communicate?

6. What feelings do you have from looking at this picture? Why?

Welcome in Bengali

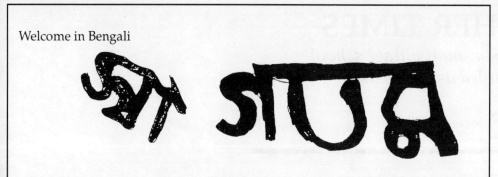

Welcome in Gujerati

chappatis

curries

dahl

and almond barfi.

The teacher encouraged the children to make accurate but positive statements when describing the spices.

The paprika smells of curry.

Nutmeg smells very strong and gingery

Mustard seeds smell very sweet.

iii) The children learnt some of the ways of preserving food. They discussed why food preservation was such an important issue.

13. Religious Education
The children learnt about the Hindu festival of Divali. They made shadow puppets to illustrate the story of Rama and Sita.

14. Culture
i) In pairs, they put on Indian garments and talked about the skills that had to be learned.

ii) The children listened to Indian music. A visit from an Indian dance troupe gave them an opportunity also to watch some Indian dancing.

iii) They learnt to write and say WELCOME in Bengali and Gujarati.

15. Display
Each group mounted an exhibition of their work and talked about it to the rest of the class.

Future Work
1. The school chose to adopt a suggestion from the parent who had come in to school to help with cooking — that all future topic work should include a 'cooking' element.

2. The children could be asked to write down two things they had learnt as a result of their work on India. These would be shared with the whole class.

3. You see a picture of starving Indian children. Write a caption or phrase that you could use to challenge this stereotype.
    e.g. Last year my mother dug irrigation channels. This year the rain never came.

Resources
Diwali Pack from Jackson Contraband (It includes slides, diva lamp, Rangoli hand patterns, incense, calendar, poster, greeting cards.)

Festivals: Diwali, Teacher's notes and pupils' worksheets. by Rosalind Kerven. MacMillan

Learning for Change in World Society : Reflections, Activities & Resources. World Studies Project. Publisher: One World Trust, 24 Palace Chambers, Bridge St., London SW1A 2JT

What is a Country? by Ange Grunsell. Oxfam Primary Education 46a Stoke Newington, Church St., London N16 0LU

Many of the OXFAM photopacks contain pictures suitable for the activities described here.

SECTION XI: OTHER PEOPLE... OTHER TIMES

By recreating the life of 18th Century itinerant pedlars, children in a small village school gained insight into the experiences of a group which could be regarded as 'outcasts'.

The Life of a 'badger' in the 18C

33

Background:

A class 0f 10-11 year olds in a voluntary aided Church of England primary school with 85 on roll.

Aims: to develop the following Concepts, Skills and Attitudes;

- interdependence
- understanding another way of life
- an awareness of the way life has changed since the 18th century and of its wide ranging and complex outcomes.
- developing a 'feel' of what it was like to be a 'Badger' in the 18th century. (The name given to intinerent hawkers in the 18th century).
- a caring attitude towards a live creature
- caring for others
- working as a team
- communication, using words and place-names of the Cumbrian dialect.
- map reading, and decision making
- developing an appreciation of another way of life.

Process:

1. Janet Niepokojczycka's journeys through history are well known locally, and feature in the local press. Her talk at a P.T.A. meeting, with slides and video, inspired the headteacher to exploit the marvellous potential of such a journey for the experiential learning of pupils.

The class used the library service and Janet's books and maps to research a similar trip with pack horses/fell ponies. They worked in pairs and small groups, planning and organising themselves for the experience. Janet and the Headteacher planned a five day route, using old pack horse tracks. The children used their map-reading skills to guide the party daily.

First, however the children spent a day learning to groom and generally care for a pony. They also checked that the 18th century costumes they chose to wear were suitable.

They also adopted forenames and last-names for the week that they felt were in keeping with 18th century, and were of Cumbrian origin. These they had turned up from their research, so they became Sarah, Margaret, Ruth, for example or Arnold and Harry.

2. The journey

The children had five ponies for the journey, two pupils to each pony. They travelled as follows:

Monday: from school via Rusland valley to Brathay Hall.

Tuesday: Brathay over Loughrigg to Elterwater Youth Hostel.

Wednesday: Loughrigg Terrace via Rydal Water/ Ambleside to Troubeck Y.H.A.

Thursday: Troutbeck to Garburn Pass on an old drover's track. On the lonely fellside the children decided to halt and to improvise imagined scenes from an 18th century badger's life. Later, at the evening stop-over they wrote and drew pictures about their experiences.

Friday: Troutbeck to Brockhole, the Lake District National Park Visitors Centre, where the children performed their plays, sold their school-made biscuits and were met by parents.

3. Plays

During the week, each group devised a short scene reflecting the life of the 'Badger': the places visited, dangers faced, and people met. The children chose the settings for their plays from the scenery on their journey. They chose places that they felt

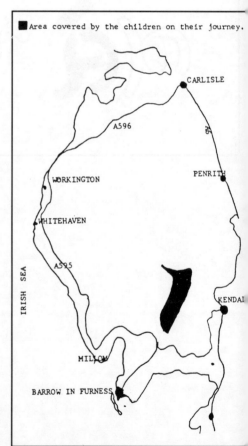

Area covered by the children on their journey.

We got our foot out of the packs. I got my
leather drinking bottle. I took a drink out.
    Although I had had it for ten years,
It tasted of leather. I had a few mouth
fulls and the man came out and said "Go.
go on you badger." And the dog barked.
I said "Don't fret I'm going." So I tied
Williams packs on and tightened up the
girth (all and I went and so did William

Boy, aged 11 years

The scent of rhododendren was strong
in the air and a Robin flitted in
its branches singing, as william cropped
grass and I got out my sandwhiches
The Robin flew over my head
and landed on an
oak still singing
its song in
those branches. Then William began
eating some bushes inside the garden
of the fence post I had had to tie him to
as there were no small trees and I went to stop him

A red face suddenly appeared at
the window of the little stone cotage
with the tiny chimney on top of
the thatched roof next to the garden
which was mainly full of vegatables.
The face then withdrew again quickly.
This looks like trouble I thought.
Then out of the house rushed a
large fat woman looking very
angry.
    "Get that horse out of here!"
she screamed.
    "Dont worry yourself," I said
"We were just going anyway."
So I packed the sacks,
tightened the girth
and put on the
leathers again and
walked off. There was
wood all around mainly oak and
birch with some sycamore and beach
mixed in.

were suitable for their performances. Each scene was put together as a final production for the parents and visitors at Brockhole. The badgers' pack-horses carried bundles of biscuits that pupils had made in school. These were sold to the visitors at Brockhole. (The children had packed them so well that not a biscuit was broken!)

4. Outsiders

The idea of 'outsiders' was brought home to the children by other people's reactions to them. On several occasions, tourists appeared very wary of the strangely clad group of children and ponies. Once they had the word 'gyppos' shouted at them.

See examples of the children's work completed on the Thursday evening stop (page 99).

5. Caring for the ponies

As the week progressed the children built up their relationships with their ponies. They came to put the well-being of their pony before other considerations, watching the tracks for sharp objects, or worrying about low overhanging branches. They paid attention to grooming and repair of the ponies' tack. Even the bells that hung around the pony's neck were checked and repaired when necessary. The children became skilled at caring for their ponies, especially at cleaning their hooves and checking that the packs were evenly weighted before loading them onto the ponies' backs.

The assumed names worked well and helped the children's empathy. They easily maintained the dialect and words like badger=hawker, wad=lead, Oregap (place-name), and traditional Cumbrian names became part of their daily conversation.

Future Work

1. The insider/outsider theme can be explored more fully through practical work and literature.

2.i) Children could discuss what role travellers such as gypsies, tramps, pedlars have in society and:

 ii) why they are marginalised;

 iii) why such people are often made scapegoats;

 iv) why we feel we need scapegoats.

TWENTIETH CENTURY 'BADGERS'.

'PAUSE FOR THOUGHT'.